DOMINO

DOMINO

·

THE SIMPLEST WAY TO INSPIRE CHANGE

·

NICK TASLER

WILEY

Published by John Wiley & Sons, Inc., Hoboken, New Jersey.
Published simultaneously in Canada.

For general information about our other products and services, please contact our Customer Care Department within the United States at (800) 762-2974, outside the United States at (317) 572-3993 or fax (317) 572-4002.

Wiley publishes in a variety of print and electronic formats and by print-on-demand. Some material included with standard print versions of this book may not be included in e-books or in print-on-demand. If this book refers to media such as a CD or DVD that is not included in the version you purchased, you may download this material at http://booksupport.wiley.com. For more information about Wiley products, visit www.wiley.com.

Library of Congress Cataloging-in-Publication Data:

Tasler, Nick, 1978-
  Domino: the simplest way to inspire change/Nick Tasler.
     pages cm
  Includes bibliographical references and index.
  ISBN 978-1-119-08306-1 (cloth); ISBN 978-1-119-08314-6 (ebk);
ISBN 978-1-119-08316-0 (ebk)
  1. Organizational change. 2. Strategic planning. I. Title.
  HD58.8.T374 2016
  658.4'063 — dc23

                                                    2015020839

Printed in the United States of America

10 9 8 7 6 5 4 3 2 1

CONTENTS

●

Contents

INTRODUCTION: WHAT'S EATING GLEN PETERSON?

•

GLEN PETERSON OPENED HIS EYES AND INSTINCTIVELY brushed the back of his thumb across his lips in a quick search to track down any stray drool unbecoming of a well-mannered adult. A scan of the other snoozing passengers in the business-class cabin told him it would still be hours before his flight from Melbourne touched down at LAX.

"Now what?" he muttered to himself.

During his two decades of international travel, Glen had developed a habit of popping two Advil PMs shortly after takeoff, which usually knocked him out until the pilot announced the final descent. But this time was different. Glen had woken up just a few hours after falling asleep. He couldn't stop thinking about a comment that Priya—one of his most trusted team members and vice president of Davis Medical's Asia-Pacific region—had made during a team dinner in Melbourne the night before.

The dinner capped off a standard two-day meeting with key leaders from the Asia-Pacific team to check in on a number of key initiatives, and to discuss the rollout of the new strategy Glen's leadership team had put together a few weeks before. Glen had his assistant arrange for dinner plans at a family-style Italian restaurant, because he liked the low-key atmosphere and always felt that the simple act of dishing your food from common bowls was a solid, if not so subtle, way to reinforce the value he placed on cohesion and collegiality among his teams.

To Glen's dismay, the meal revealed more confusion than cohesion.

When the heaping dishes of food were placed on the center of the table, everyone just sat there for a moment staring at the massive spread of edible options, trying to decide where to begin. That's when Priya leaned over to Glen.

"It's funny," she said.

"What's that?" Glen had asked with a big smile, his eyes still fixed on the feast before them.

"I always get slightly nervous when I eat at a place like this." She shook her head and smiled sheepishly. "I look at all this delicious food, and I know that my stomach will not afford me all the space I need to try everything. So I have to choose wisely in the beginning, or I might not make it to the very best entrees."

"I know *exactly* what you mean!" Glen laughed. "Unfortunately for me," he said while patting his stomach, "I think I have a little *too much* spare room for sampling these days."

"Perhaps," Priya chuckled. Then her eyes narrowed. "Our new plan for the business is kind of like that," she said. "We have all these different bowls laid out before us, each of them filled up with heaps of initiatives and deliverables. It all looks so delicious and exciting, but something about it also makes me slightly nervous."

"Yeah, I guess anytime we do something new it is always a little exciting and a little nerve-wracking at the same time, isn't it?" Glen said.

"Yes, I suppose so," Priya continued. "But Glen, I think my concern about this plan is about more than just the anxiety of doing something new."

"Okay, now you've got me curious," Glen said. "Please do continue."

"It seems as though we have identified some rather significant changes to the way we want to do things in the coming year, correct?"

"Yes, you could certainly say that," Glen said.

"Well, I shared the plan with a couple of my savvier team members, James and Caroline, and—"

"Of course. I like them both a lot," Glen said. "Caroline in particular always impresses me."

"Yes, they are both very bright, Glen. That's what concerns me."

"Wait. You're *concerned* that you have two really bright team members? I think we need to give you more things to worry about," Glen said with a grin.

Priya laughed.

"I'm sorry," Glen said. "I interrupted you. Please go on. What concerns you?"

"Well, I asked them to explain the new plan to me the way they thought they would explain it to their own teams, and to tell me how they would go about their work differently each day given this new strategy. I wanted to test the plan on them—to see what stood out to them and . . . ," Priya looked away for a moment, searching for the right words.

Glen leaned in. "And . . . ?"

"They are two of the highest performers we have in our department and they almost completely missed the most critical changes to our plan this year. I suppose it's not fair to say that they 'missed' the changes. They did *mention* them. But I believe they missed the *significance* of the changes, and the implications for what they should be doing this year. The core of our plan is different in very important ways compared to what we've been doing in prior months. We are going to produce devices for a new target market that we've consciously avoided for as long as I've been with the company. To succeed, we really need our best people on the front lines thinking creatively every day about the new direction so they can spot the opportunities you and I can't see from our vantage point."

"Absolutely," Glen confirmed. "No question that we'll have to shift our focus."

"But . . . *are we*?" Priya's eyes shifted upward as she searched again for the right words. "Does our plan truly reflect a change in focus?"

Glen looked puzzled as Priya let her question hang there. "I *think* so," he said with a twinge of uncertainty in his voice.

"Glen, you know that I fully believe in our new direction. It's just that we produce so many new features and products every year that I'm afraid our people won't fully grasp why this one is different. This product fundamentally alters the terms of our relationships with customers. The margins will be different. The value proposition will be different. And James and Caroline don't fully comprehend how this plan changes much about what they do each day. They believe that their basic goals and priorities are the same as last year and the year before, plus with only the small addition of a couple of more priorities.

"And to be honest, Glen, I believe they are disappointed. James and Caroline can see the same opportunities that those of us on the leadership team identified at the planning retreat. They know how much healthcare reform is going to change the way we need to do business. And I think they were actually hoping for something a bit more . . . *radical* than the plan we produced. A plan that is undeniably different from previous years. They want to see a change as much as we do, but . . . well, they just aren't seeing it in the plan we've presented to them."

Glen felt his cheeks turning crimson. A decade or so ago, Glen might have snapped back with a pithy defense of the plan. He would sharply suggest that perhaps Priya just hadn't articulated the plan correctly. But with years of conscious effort Glen had trained himself to take a deep breath first in order to give his rational brain a chance to grab the tail of his lizard brain before it spewed out a conversation-killing rebuttal. After a moment, he realized that even if Priya hadn't presented the plan clearly enough, the failure was still *his* failure because it meant that *he* hadn't articulated it clearly enough to her.

"Hm. That's interesting," he said. To buy himself a few moments for collecting his thoughts, Glen reached for the fettuccine bowl and scooped some onto his plate. As he dug the spoon back into the pile of pasta, the untouched quinoa (pronounced "KEEN-wah") dish in the center of the table caught his eye. Then it hit him. *Quinoa*, he thought to himself. His wife had just recently introduced him to this so-called ancient grain that looked a lot like rice to him. But she explained that it was a healthier alternative to most of the standard pastas for which he had a lifelong weakness. He determined that a little extra quinoa would probably do his diet some good. So, tonight Glen had ordered quinoa in addition to the lasagna, the fettuccine Alfredo, the spaghetti bolognese, and the other staple Italian dishes.

That was the problem.

Glen slowly shook his head. "You're absolutely right. The changes to our plan are like the quinoa."

Priya raised a curious eyebrow and cocked her head to the side.

"The strategic shifts we've made are going to get lost in the smorgasbord of ongoing initiatives. We'll get things done this year, efficiently and effectively, just like we always do. But they won't be the *right* things . . . or at least not enough of the new things that are going to move us in that new direction." Glen paused and let out a big exhale. "I just assumed that simply ordering the quinoa would not only make *me* eat it, but that everyone else would notice something new on the table, and also dig right in.

"But they won't, will they?" Glen asked rhetorically. "Purely out of habit, they are going to reach for the stuff they have always reached for—the quality assurance guidelines, the margin increases, the supply chain improvements . . . all the stuff we talked about last year. And I won't be able to blame them, because a few months ago those *were* the right answers."

Priya nodded. "That's what I'm afraid of, yes." She dug a serving spoon into the quinoa dish. "Somehow we have to get our people to instinctively reach for these new key objectives *first*. And I'm afraid that six to eight months from now will be too late. As quickly as things are changing, Glen, I'm afraid we might have to pursue another new set of priorities two or three more times before this year is even over."

Now, 35,000 feet into the night sky somewhere over the black abyss of the Pacific Ocean, Glen Peterson sat in silence. His conversation with Priya played on repeat in his mind. Every time, like a scratch on a disc, the dialogue stops at the same spot: *six to eight months from now will be too late.*

He looked out the window at the darkness. "What are we missing?" he thought. All the pieces were in place. All the dominoes were lined up. What else could he possibly do to get them to start falling?

Glen slipped on his reading glasses and scrolled through his strategic planning documents on his iPad. After briefly flipping through the slide deck he had presented to the corporate planning committee, he scrolled down the projections spreadsheets looking for some kind of clue, some sort of hint about where to go next. When his eyes drifted down to the spreadsheet's twelfth row titled "inPulse acquisition" he paused.

inPulse was the flagship product of a startup device maker that Davis Medical had just acquired. It was a good product that had already passed nearly all its clinic trials. But Glen and his team realized it could be much more than that. The inPulse products were designed for an altogether different customer group than Davis' traditional customers. Unlike virtually all of Davis' hundreds of other devices, inPulse was a product that fell squarely on the value-side of the so-called "volume-to-value revolution" in healthcare. That meant that the inPulse project could be a powerful symbol of the new direction in which Glen wanted to take his division.

Yet James and Caroline—the canaries in his division's coal mine—barely even noticed it on the plan. How much clearer could he make it? After a few moments staring at the words "inPulse acquistion" Glen looked up from his tablet.

"Could it really be that simple?" he wondered to himself.

His squinted eyes slowly began to open wider as the answer took shape in his mind. He was beginning to feel that old, familiar surge of dopamine flood his brain—the one that so often transformed his anxiety into excitement, and reminded him why he loved his work.

He quickly slid his iPad over to the edge of the tray table, and leaned ahead to reach under his seat for the pen and the yellow legal pad that he always carried in his tote bag.

At the top of the legal pad, he scribbled "quinoa = inPulse" and circled it.

Then a few lines below that he wrote "Fettuccine = _____." He paused for a few more seconds to think before scribbling down "market intell." on the blank line. Then he wrote "supply chain effic. proj." and then "X-cath. quality enhancements" underneath that.

quinoa = inPulse

fettuccine = <u>market intell.</u>

   supply chain effic. proj.

   X-cath. quality enhancements

That was it. If he could just make it clear that not only was the inPulse acquisition a top priority for the next year, but then call out the specific projects that were now a *lower* priority it might just send the unmistakable message to his team that something important had changed. And his decision might just trigger a domino effect of decisions that would shift the focus of his entire division in a matter of weeks, if not days.

●

THE LEADER WITH A THOUSAND FACES

To paraphrase the writer Joseph Campbell, Glen Peterson is the leader with a thousand faces. Glen's story is *your* story. Whether you run a Fortune 500 company, lead a hospital unit, manage a project team, own a small business, or temporarily preside over a parent-teacher association, you have almost certainly faced the challenge of inspiring a group of people to shift their focus quick enough to pursue a new set of objectives, sidestep a new threat, or seize a new opportunity. The protagonist here, Glen P., is actually a pseudonym for any

Great Leader Executing a New Plan. He is an amalgam of the real leaders you'll read about in the following pages.

There are two ways for a Glen P. to approach change. You can change by addition or you can change by decision. The Latin root of the word "decide" is *caidere*, which means to kill or to cut (think: homicide, suicide, genocide). Technically, deciding to do something new without cutting something old is not a decision at all. It is merely an *addition*.

Change by addition is the hard way. It complicates plans, distracts leaders, frustrates team members, and pretty much guarantees that nobody will eat the quinoa. Not only is change by addition painfully slow, it also promotes nightly bouts of sheep counting when you would rather be sleeping.

Change by decision is the simple way.

Decisions are the most fundamental building blocks of change. Change stalls precisely because those decisions aren't happening—at the top, in the middle, or somewhere on the front lines.

After his conversation with Priya, Glen Peterson realized that he was adding new priorities on top of old priorities. By the time you finish reading *Domino*, you'll see that the answer to Glen's question "could it really be that simple?" is "yes." Inspiring people to change directions really is that simple. Contrary to what most of us have been conditioned to believe, inspiring change doesn't require uncommon intelligence, a charismatic personality, a complicated plan, or even an awe-inspiring vision. The truth is much simpler. It's not magic. It's a combination of science and common sense. All the stories and all the research you'll discover in this book point to one simple truth.

If you can make a decision, you can inspire change.

●

SHARP TURNS AND WIDE CURVES

Assume for a second that you're on your way across town for one of your kids' birthday parties. You are just coming home from work in your car and your husband has the kids with him in the minivan. You know the way to the party, but your husband does not, so you'll have to lead him there. Along the way, you'll have to lead him around two kinds of turns.

One kind of turn will involve following the curves in a winding road. These curves are in plain sight, and everyone knows they are coming for miles in advance. Unmistakable signs leading up to the curve say "winding road ahead." Then, when you get a little closer, more signs say "curve ahead." Then, just before you come to the bend, a sign will say something like "slow down for curve." Even if your daydreaming husband missed all of those other signs, it is virtually impossible to miss the whole series of bright yellow arrow signs pointing directly to the curve while you round it. As if that weren't enough, the actual pavement rounding the curve is slanted downward in a way that practically forces your husband's tires to turn without him even moving the steering wheel. The road is literally turning with him around the curve.

An intersection requires a different kind of turn. This time the road doesn't help you out. In fact the road almost dares your husband to keep going straight like the rest of the traffic is doing. So if ol' daydream believer is too busy singing along with Taylor Swift or ruminating over his fantasy football lineup to notice you switch lanes and turn, then he is going to miss the turn. That means you're going to end up at Chuck E. Cheez's all by yourself. Nobody wants that.

Most "change management" in big corporations is devoted to the kinds of change that resemble a curve in the road. These are choice-less changes. They include things like software upgrades, reorganizations, and mergers or acquisitions. On Friday you logged into the old software system, and on Monday morning you logged into the new one. Love it? Hate it? Doesn't matter. The old system simply doesn't exist anymore. One day the sign above your office building said "Wachovia" and the next day it said "Wells Fargo." (Ah ha! So that's what all the sawdust, orange tape, and blatant dress code violations were all about during the past six months. It wasn't a Village People revival after all!) The curve came and went and you didn't really have to do anything except show up. Even if the people following you around this curve are not paying any attention at all, those changes still happen. Of course, they are easier if you get "buy-in" from your team. But one way or another, the change happens.

I'm not saying those changes are easy. But I am saying that those changes are impossible to miss because the road itself turns. You have to intentionally drive off the road in order to miss that change in direction.

But not all changes work like that. When you switch lanes or turn the corner at an intersection, the people behind you have to consciously decide to follow you instead of continuing to go straight. These changes are choice-dependent—the people following you have to intentionally decide to turn with you. If you don't get their attention, they'll fly right by you. These are the strategic shifts that are becoming more and more essential for leaders at all levels of an organization.

So how do you make sure the people behind you stay with you while making these more subtle turns?

First, you have to get your followers' attention, and let them know which direction you plan to go. That's why you signal your turn by using the "blinker" on your car. It tells the cars behind you, "Hey, I've made a decision. I'm not going to keep going this direction anymore. Instead I'm going to turn soon, and when I do I'll be turning right and not left."

Second, you have to check your rearview mirror to verify that the people following you have decided that they too are going to turn. Since you can't read their minds you have to constantly check your mirrors to see if they have in fact turned on their own blinkers. If you don't see their blinker flash on, then you know you need to slow down and make sure you have their attention before you arrive at the intersection.

Use your blinker. Check your mirrors. You can do that right? Yes, I thought so. Your mother was right. You are special.

At the risk of spoiling the rest of the book—yes it's *that* good—here's what you can expect. The first section, Driving Change, is all about making decisions that signal a turn or a lane change for your group. You'll discover how to make those decisions, how to help your team stay with you during the change, and the research that explains why this is all so darned effective. You'll also learn how to conduct a proper permission ceremony, orchestrate a 90-day sprint, and create a series of waitlists for all that clutter—er, I mean, for all those important initiatives that need to be put on hold in order to drive home the change.

In the final section, Adapt to Change, we'll zoom out so you can see how these core principles lay the foundation for a more agile way of doing what your team needs to do every day, regardless of any official "change initiatives." Because, let's face it, when is the last time you weren't either trying to cope with, or planning to drive, some kind of change? As soon as today's change is over, there will be two more changes waiting to take its place. Change is to leadership what water is to fish.

So without further ado, let's start eating, driving, swimming, and mixing more metaphors.

PART ONE

•

Drive Change

•

SECTION I

•

Use Your Blinkers

•

1

•

Sandy's Rule

•

A FEW YEARS AGO, I WAS ASKED to give a talk at a global sales conference for a multinational technology company. In response to plateauing sales, the leadership team defined a change strategy to reignite their growth. Unfortunately, they had announced the change nearly nine months before and it hadn't taken hold. With the conference only two weeks away, they were hoping I could help.

In cases like this where I'm hearing about a session just days before the event, my job more closely resembles triage than it does consulting or speaking. Since that happens fairly often, I've had to develop some shortcuts to get my arms around a situation quickly. One of these shortcuts involves writing the word NEW at the top of a blank notebook page. Then about halfway down the page I scribble the word OLD. As the clients explain their vision of the future to me, I begin taking notes under NEW. If my notes fill up the space between NEW and OLD before they finish explaining their plan, it's often a good sign that we need to clarify the strategy. I adhere to Einstein's dictum that "if you can't explain it to a six-year-old, you don't understand it yourself." As my wife will attest, I play the part of a six-year-old disturbingly well so this method lets me leverage my gift of perennial immaturity. I've found that if I can understand the vision after just a few minutes, then it is usually crystal clear to the client's team members.

So when this call began, I opened my notebook and jotted down NEW then OLD on a blank page. After a few minutes of small talk I asked them to tell me about the new strategy.

"What is it all about?" I said.

The group's vice president, whom we'll call "Sandy," jumped in to explain how the new plan focused on something called "co-selling." Essentially, their internal salespeople would start working closely with the company's external distributors with whom they'd traditionally had more of what you might call a *frenemy* relationship. In theory, they are on the same team, but in practice there was an unspoken assumption that the external distributors might cannibalize your sales, and therefore your paycheck.

With co-selling the idea is that external distributors better understand the individual customer's challenges, while the internal salespeople at the company that actually makes the products better understand the range of possible solutions to offer said customers. By working together, they are able to recommend a more fitting solution to address each customer's unique challenges. Makes sense, right?

When Sandy finished explaining, I had plenty of room to spare between NEW and OLD.

So far so good.

A decade ago, I would have stopped right there and moved on to discuss the demographics of the group, the logistics of the conference, and other housekeeping matters. After all, the new vision was vivid and concise. It was crystal clear *why* the change needed to happen. Everyone understood what "co-selling" was and how to do it. And we had no reason to believe that they somehow lacked the skills or abilities to do it. This was textbook change management.

There was just one problem. They had launched the new initiative seven months before and nothing had changed.

"That sounds great," I continued. "So let's move on now to what needs to change."

Silence.

After a few awkward moments, Sandy spoke up and very patiently explained it to me again. "You see, Nick, with the new model our people will be partnering with the distributors to really figure out what the customers' *true* challenges are so that we can provide them with a comprehensive solution that better suits them."

"Ah, okay, I think I get it. So provide comprehensive solutions as opposed to . . . *what*?" I asked.

More silence.

I broke the verbal stalemate this time. "Sorry, I am not being very clear here," I said. "Let me try again. What have your people been doing that you want them to *quit* doing so that they can do all the new things that co-selling requires of them?"

At that point, it finally sunk in. They were adding new priorities on top of old priorities, rather than replacing the old objectives. They were touting new behaviors, but not explicitly killing or even reducing any old behaviors. They were trying to be in the old place and the new place both at the same time. As a result, the whole department was either oblivious or confused or frustrated or all of the above.

Meanwhile the clock was still ticking on all the department's goals for the year.

The top leaders couldn't understand why their people weren't jumping onboard.

Tick . . . tick . . . tick. . . .

The middle managers couldn't imagine how they were expected to take on the extra work required of co-selling without a bigger team and a bigger budget. As far as they knew, they still had to perform all the old duties, but now had a whole bunch of new responsibilities on top of them.

Tick . . . tick . . . tick. . . .

The salespeople out on the front lines could sense the tension between their direct managers and the executive leadership. This just confirmed the belief that their bosses were nice enough people, but were largely ineffectual cogs in the corporate wheel incapable of talking sense to the out-of-touch executives who didn't really understand what it was like "in the field." So the salesforce simply shook their heads, shrugged their shoulders, and assured each other that this newest fad too shall pass. Back to business as usual.

Tick . . . tick . . . tick. . . .

Fortunately, this was a talented team with a legitimately strong plan in place. Once we correctly identified the problem, the solution was simple.

●

ATTENTION + DIRECTION = CHANGE

"I think that's it," Sandy said. "I've sent out multiple emails and voicemails announcing the new emphasis on co-selling. We've even brought in outside trainers to conduct co-selling courses to our sales teams. They 'get it.' But the message hasn't hit home yet, it hasn't translated to action yet. Now I think I know why."[1]

"Really? Why do you think that is?" I asked her.

"It's the old versus new thing. I don't know that we've made that clear. I think we—those of us on the leadership team, I mean—just assumed that the change was . . . obvious."

"How so?" I said

"I agree with you, Sandy," said Michael, one of Sandy's directors and the organizer of the upcoming conference. "I think everyone gets what co-selling is. They just aren't sure exactly what they need to put on hold or quit doing altogether. A lot of the people on our team probably *think* they are co-selling. And from time to time, I think they are actually involving the distributors in the process. But it's hard to tell, because just as often, they are calling on their customers by themselves and leaving the distributor out of the loop."

"And why do you think that is?" I asked.

"They just don't think it's necessary in a lot of instances," Michael said. "I can say from personal experience, it feels that way a lot. Typically, a big chunk of our sales come from license renewals on our software—and often that just means getting customer organizations to pay for the unlicensed software that their people have been using illegally all along. It's pretty basic. Those kinds of sales just don't require much outside help to make."

"So if that is where most of your sales come from, and they don't require co-selling, then why are you transitioning to co-selling?" I asked.

"Correction. That's where our sales *used to* come from," Michael explained. "Things are changing, though. We can't rely on those license renewals to maintain our position anymore, let alone to *grow*. The perception in the marketplace is that we've become 'piracy police' instead of trusted partners or solution-providers."

"That's it then, isn't it, Michael?" Sandy asked rhetorically. "It's the licensing deals that need to get cut."

"Well . . . I suppose . . . *maybe* . . . ," Michael stammered.

"I don't mean cut them out altogether," Sandy clarified. "We'd go out of business if we did that. I just mean we need to make an example out of the licensing deals—to show the team just how serious we are about co-selling as our future, and how the things we did before aren't going to work anymore."

"What do you think your people would say if you did that— told them to 'stop selling licensing deals,' I mean?" I asked her.

Sandy laughed. "They would think we lost our bloody minds!"

"Well, that's a good thing," I said, only half-joking. "That's what we want. Crazy people get other people's attention."

"Oh, it would *definitely* get their attention!" Michael said.

"But okay. I get it," I said. "So you can't ax all efforts toward selling licensing deals, but—"

"No, we couldn't," Sandy interrupted. "That would bankrupt us. But what we could do is change the proportions. Michael, about what percent of your team's sales have come from license renewals this year?"

"I don't know. I'd guess probably 60 to 70 percent."

"So assuming that is representative of everyone else, how about we introduce something like a '51 percent rule'? At least 51 percent of your sales must come from something other than licensing deals. You'll receive higher bonuses for reaching that ratio, and be penalized for missing it."

Michael let out an audible sigh into the phone. "I'll be honest," he said. "That gives me a mini panic attack." He paused for a moment, then continued, "but on the other hand, it would definitely cause me to rethink my team's approach."

"Well, that's the point, isn't it," Sandy said. "We have to send a signal that we are serious about changing immediately."

"Yes, I guess. I mean, yes, you're right. That is the point," Michael concurred.

I don't want to be too callous since we were talking about real people's livelihoods. But one litmus test for determining whether or not you've actually made a change *decision* or just a change *addition* is whether the people on your team feel any discomfort. If there isn't any discomfort, chances are that you haven't really made a decision. I once heard change described this way: *change is loss; loss is pain.* If there is no initial pain, then there is no loss. If there is no loss, then there is no change.

That's not just pop psychology either. It speaks to one of the most reliable phenomena in human psychology called "loss aversion." Loss aversion[2] was identified in a series of studies back in the 1970s by Nobel laureate Daniel Kahneman and his colleague Amos Tversky. It has since been replicated in thousands of studies in every situation imaginable from shopping and dating to working and investing. The simple fact is that people hate loss. Actually, "people" is too limiting. Research shows that even fish in the seas, birds in the trees, not to mention apes in the jungles and . . . okay, I can't think of a habitat that rhymes with "ungle," but you get the point. Loss aversion is universal. That's why we hold on to poor-performing employees long after it's time to let them go. That's why we "throw good money after bad" when making investments. That's why we so often fail to strive for the job we really want, because we are afraid of losing the security or prestige or comfort that comes from the mildly unsatisfying job we already have. The prospect of losing security or influence or comfort causes a sharp and instinctive emotional reaction. Eventually, good judgment from the rational part of our brain can in fact overrule that knee jerk—and often irrational— aversion to loss, but it's almost impossible to eliminate the reaction before it happens. So if there is no "mini panic attack" like Michael's, then there probably won't be any change either.

The good news is that this emotional reaction is part of what wakes people up. It's what gets their attention and signals a turn. But aren't there other ways to get people's attention?

Sandy could have shown up wearing a hard hat and a utility belt, and asked the rest of her leadership team to dress up as the other members of the Village People, then kicked off the session with a rendition of *YMCA*. She could have reenacted a scene from *Dead Poets Society* by jumping up on a table while reading off the strategic plan for the year, and then asked her team to reply with "Oh captain, my captain!" She could have done wind sprints in her pumps on stage at the global sales conference. At the very least, she could have sent out a mass voicemail to her department that began with a really funny joke before launching into the new priorities. Any of those communications would have been unexpected, memorable, and attention-grabbing.

But none of those elaborate distractions would have been as effective as publicly deciding which of the other known, recognized priorities would be burnt as a sacrifice on the altar of the new strategic direction. What a decision does that a great joke or a silly costume won't do is to clarify a direction that the rest of the team can use to make decisions for themselves.

That's why change *decisions* function like a blinker, and change *additions* function like hazard lights. With a turn signal, the blinking light only flashes on one side of the car at a time — either the left side or the right side. Unlike every other light on a car, a blinker has to get people's attention *and* signal a change in a specific direction. When the car in front of you slams on its brakes, its brake lights illuminate immediately so that you know to slow down. When the driver in front of you switches on the hazard lights, it also gets your attention and tells you to be alert because something is going wrong with that car. But you don't really know what's going on. Are they turning? Did their brakes go out? Did they blow a tire? Do they need help? Did their toddler toss a smartphone out the window? So you might worry, slow down, and gawk, but you'll basically keep right on moving down the road just like before . . . only slower.

What makes the blinkers different from the brake lights or the hazard lights is that blinkers also clearly indicate the new direction.

For leaders who identify a necessary change, the instinctive temptation is to switch on their hazard lights, instead of their blinkers. Sandy had talked herself hoarse for the previous year warning her team about the need to refocus their efforts. She desperately tried to get their attention. And her team wasn't dumb. They knew that the old model of selling wasn't long for this world. But without a clear decision about which old priorities they should temporarily quit pursuing, all those passionate pleas and bold pronouncements in emails, speeches, and voicemails presented the new direction as an *addition* rather than as a decision.

By now, you've probably heard about the famous psychology study[3] where psychologists Daniel Simons and Christopher Chabris asked participants to watch a video of a group of people passing a basketball back and forth, and then count how many passes they make. A few seconds into the video a guy in a gorilla suit walks behind them, faces the camera, pounds his chest a few times, and then walks off the set again. (If you aren't familiar with the study, it's about . . . well, what you just read.)

Most of the participants were so busy diligently counting the passes of the basketball that they didn't even notice Donkey Kong stroll through behind them.

Your new strategic direction is like the guy in the gorilla suit. All your other priorities, key objectives, and projects-in-progress are like the basketball players passing the ball. Pounding your chest with ACTION REQUIRED emails will not get their attention until you tell them it's okay—and, in fact, expected—for them to *stop counting passes*. Telling them to look out for the gorilla, without explicitly ordering them to stop counting passes for a moment, doesn't cause them to change. It causes them to multitask. It inspires overwork, exhaustion, and burnout. But it doesn't inspire change.

When Sandy announced the 51 percent rule at the conference, it effectively sent the team a pitch-perfect message that both got their attention *and* pointed to the new direction by forsaking the old direction.

Another variation of Sandy's 51 percent rule was applied by a clever human resources director I work with. In response to a larger culture change, the HR leader wanted to get his department to think differently about their role in the company. Internal surveys showed that most managers throughout the company viewed the HR department like an internal police force. They were the "compliance cops." That's because the only time most of the managers ever interacted with their HR representative was when they wanted permission for firing someone, or to deal with some employee complaint about their management behavior.

As a result, the managers' relationships with HR had become an elaborate game of cat and mouse. Managers spent more time cleverly devising ways to escape the notice of HR than they did trying to figure out how to make the right people-management decisions.

For their part, some of the people in HR actually liked this relationship. It made them feel powerful. It made them feel like crusaders of truth and justice whose job was to protect the little guy from the evil bosses. It was a case of noble intentions resulting in ignoble behavior.

So how would you go about inspiring a change like this? How do you change a time-worn relationship that was being reinforced from both sides every day for decades?

The HR leader made a decision. He decided to ban the word "no" from his department's vocabulary. "Never say no" became the mantra of the department.

Think about what this simple rule accomplished. Without the ability to say "no," the HR representatives were forced to interact completely differently with the managers in the field. Now, when asked whether or not they could fire an employee, the HR rep had to say something like "N—I mean . . . well, let's see. Uh, here's what we're facing legally if you terminate this person without proper documentation. So I would say definitely N—er, I mean, what's *your* opinion?"

Suddenly, the ball was back in the manager's court. No longer was the manager engaged in a chess match with the HR rep to see what he could get away with. It became a joint problem-solving session, where the manger got to tap into expert advice on the implications and consequences of each option. Instead of being the cop, the HR rep was now more like the manager's personal legal counsel. Not only did the icy relations between HR and management begin to thaw, the managers also started to become better decision makers. They were now forced to think through what the right choice should be, instead of thinking only about how to "get away with" doing whatever it is they wanted to do. At the same time, the conversations gave the HR reps a deeper understanding of the managers' points of view. They had to hear why this employee was causing a problem for the business, and in order to understand that reasoning, the HR reps were forced to better understand the business side of the equation, and look beyond the HR worldview.

Another perfectly rational (though flawed) way to approach this change would have been to come up with a script to guide every interaction. First, you define the problem. "Ms. Manager, what's the real issue here?" Second, you ask, "Do you understand the implications of this decision?" Then you say, "What do you think we should do in this situation?"

That approach makes perfect sense, but it won't get anyone's attention. It won't make anyone change. Why? Because it sounds way too much like every other yawn-inducing training curriculum on customer service or interpersonal communications they've had. On top of that, it feels like it only makes their jobs more complicated. *Now, in addition to everything else I have to remember every day, I also have to memorize this plastic, artificial sounding set of questions that everyone knows is fake and not really "me." Ugh.*

The "never say no" rule took a very different approach. It was a decision, and not an addition. It didn't add a bunch of new skills or lists of behaviors that must be learned and memorized. It simply kicked out a crutch that the entire department had leaned on for years, instead of changing.

The rule also grabbed the HR department's attention precisely because of the risks it conjured up in their minds. The first thing everyone thought of was, "But if we never say no, the company is going to get sued every other day! You should hear some of the stuff that these managers try to get away with!" It was that shock—that potential loss—that grabbed everyone's attention and finally sparked a productive conversation about a real change.

In truth, all the rule really did was put more accountability on the managers' shoulders. It also removed a veil of cover from those managers who were truly poor leaders, but had been able to hide under the protection of this contentious relationship with HR. If the company got sued because that manager made a rash decision, the manager knew that he now shared equally in the responsibility for that decision. Also, the HR reps had to learn to be influential and to think strategically, instead of being authoritarian and narrow-minded. This was the ultimate direction that the head of HR wanted the department to move all along. But simply saying, "Be more influential, instead of authoritarian," even really loudly, was a statement that had no teeth. It was vague and ambiguous and failed to inspire true change. Only when he made the decision to cut out the word "no" from the human resources lexicon did the team finally begin to change.

2
•

Why the Principal Killed the Football Team

•

ONE FRIDAY AFTERNOON IN SEPTEMBER A FEW years ago, high school students in the rural south Texas town of Premont gathered for a pep rally. Teenaged giggles, creaky bleachers, and the smell of stale popcorn and sweat socks filled the air of the old Premont High School gymnasium. Meanwhile the painted-faced students cheered and shook their noisemakers, releasing the week's pent-up energy in a collective display of school spirit.

On first glance, the casual observer would not have seen anything especially unusual. Sure, the building looked a bit outdated. But then again, most rural school buildings outside the reach of fast-growing suburban areas are outdated. What's new? All things considered, this gathering would look pretty much the same as the thousands of other Friday afternoon pep rallies happening all around America that autumn—the kind of pep rallies that you and I remember going to during our school years.

But if the observer stuck around for a little while, she would notice something conspicuously absent. High school boys in red Premont Cowboy football jerseys were nowhere to be found. Later that night—and every other Friday night that fall—the only people you would find on the grass inside the run-down Jimmy Livingston Football Stadium were a few 9- or 10-year-old kids and their dads prepping the field for the next morning's peewee football games.

Eventually the observer would have to ask the obvious question.

Where is the football team?

In January of that year, the Premont Independent School District had been sentenced to death by the Texas Education Association. After years of financial trouble, dismal academic performance, and laughable student attendance at school, the state's governing body informed Premont Independent School District that they had six months to wrap up their affairs before shuttering the town's entire school system from kindergarten through twelfth grade: the same school system that educated the current student body's parents years earlier, and their parents' parents decades before that. They were now just weeks away from boarding up the only educational institution the town had ever known.

But the town had resolved to fight. That meant someone needed to turn things around. Fast. And not just *some* things. There was the overwhelming budget deficit. The rowdy students. The failing teachers. The dilapidated facilities.

"I've been in hundreds of classrooms," the school district's new superintendent Ernest Singleton told the *Atlantic Monthly*. "This was the worst I've seen in my career. The kids were in control. The language was filthy. The teachers were not prepared."

In response to the crisis, Singleton and the other administrators began making sweeping changes. They closed down the middle school building and moved all the students to the high school building. They laid off eight employees. They sealed off the mold-infested science labs at the high school. They continued plodding along without a music teacher or an art teacher at the elementary school. They started requiring students to wear uniforms. They gave teachers extra time for training and planning. They revamped the curriculum to align with the increasingly rigorous state standards.

Yet, it still wasn't enough.

In spite of the downsizing and the facilities shuffling, the cultural issues—the hearts and minds and behaviors—at the root of Premont's problems were not changing. The same students and teachers and coaches were still doing basically the same things they always did. The only thing that had really changed was that now everyone—students and teachers alike— were forced to somehow deliver more results with fewer resources and less space. (Sound familiar?) Morale at the school and in the Premont community hit an all-time low.

What Singleton did next floored the townspeople and made national headlines. He suspended football.[1]

To be clear, Singleton suspended almost all sports at Premont, and not just football. But eliminating a high school football program in rural Texas is like . . . well, eliminating high school football in rural Texas.

"I knew the minute I announced it, it would be like the world had caved in on us," Singleton said. Many felt it was the death-blow to a community that was already on life support. Two teachers quit. Fifteen students transferred. The townspeople were outraged. And then just when it seemed like things couldn't get worse, something sudden and unexpected happened.

The people of Premont changed.

A few weeks after the decision to suspend football, one hundred sixty parents showed up to the 2011–2012 school year's parent-teacher night, in contrast with a grand total of *six* parents the year before. In past years, a fight in the school hallways broke out at least once every other week. In the first 12 weeks that year, there had yet to be a single student brawl. Even the former football coach who had his team pulled out from under him couldn't help but notice the change. "Learning is going on in 99 percent of the classrooms now, compared to only 2 percent before," he said. Thirty percent more students passed their classes that semester compared to the previous year's first semester.

Premont's quarterback-in-waiting, a junior named Nathan, who was robbed of the opportunity to play football his junior and senior seasons, noted, "It did make you focus. There was just all this extra time. You never got behind on your work."

More free time, and some breathing room on the budget certainly helped. But the decision to suspend sports did more than save money or create extra time. It accomplished something far more valuable to the people of Premont. It got their attention. A disgruntled cheerleader and eventual valedictorian, Maria Navarro, bluntly explained: "We were freaking out."

●

As it turns out, getting people's attention is something that decisions—*real* decisions as opposed to additions masquerading as decisions—are uniquely qualified to do.

But why?

Right around the same time as the town of Premont was enduring its first Friday night without football, my company Decision Pulse began a series of field experiments designed to help teams get better aligned.

The experiments were simple. We would spend a few hours with a team to help them clarify what their primary goal was for the year. Then every couple of weeks for the next three months every person on each team anonymously submitted a decision they had made in pursuit of that goal they defined. Finally the rest of the team members would vote for one of their peer's decisions that they thought was best.

The purpose of this exercise was simply to take a big, often abstract team or organizational goal—like "increase customer enrollments," "get compliant with the new government regulation," or just "increase employee engagement"—and make it relevant and actionable for every person as quickly as possible, regardless of their role in the company. The peer-voting process required people to think critically about how their peers in the exact same environment were interpreting and applying that goal to their everyday actions.

We hypothesized that they would take that learning from their peers and apply it to their own work.

To our pleasant surprise, the process worked even better than expected. By the second or third round, virtually all the participants on each of the teams "got it." They understood what their organization's goal meant for their team and their daily tasks, and then started making decisions that aligned with that goal.

Sweet victory.

But we also discovered something else.

After seeing the voting results on hundreds of decisions from different teams in different organizations representing a variety of industries, we started to see a pattern. There was something inherently different about the decisions that received the most votes compared with all the others.

See if you can spot the difference. Look at the actions below from a sample group of real managers at a health insurance provider that had just launched a plan aimed at expanding the company's customer base.

Manager A: *I dealt with an employee relations issue through direct coaching and performance management versus letting that customer service manager ignore the issue.*

Manager B: *I cut out layers of security for the new customer portal because it would make it slower for customers to access.*

Manager C: *I chose to market the company as the leader of good health, not just for the current members, but for everyone.*

On first glance, there doesn't seem to be anything unique or different about any one of these actions. If I asked you to vote which one you thought would contribute most to the company's new plan, which one would you vote for?

When we showed a group of managers inside this company these three decisions above along with the 15 other decisions from other managers, Manager B's choice overwhelmingly received the most votes. Over half the managers anonymously and independently voted for Manager B's decision.

In contrast, guess how many people voted for Manager A or Manager C? Zero.

Why?

Decisions like the one from Manager B are so much more effective at refocusing people's attention because of the way our brains make sense of new information, and because of what happens when a new piece of information *does not* make sense.

In a classic study, the psychologists Jerome Brunner and Leo Postman[2] (both then at Harvard University) sat people down at a table and showed them playing cards one at a time. Most of the cards were just like you and I would expect them to be. Some were red. Some were black. Some had numbers, while others had pictures of cartoon royalty. Some of them had images of black clubs or black spades, and others showed pictures of red diamonds or red hearts.

But every now and then the researchers pulled up specially made trick cards. They showed the participants a misfit card like a queen of diamonds that was black instead of red. To the researcher's astonishment, participants responded with what Brunner and Postman described as "acute personal stress."

One participant exclaimed, "I can't make the suit out whatever it is. It didn't even look like a card that time. I don't know what color it is now or whether it's a spade or a heart. I'm not even sure what a spade looks like. My God!"

Mind you, this was not the World Series of Poker. The participants had no money riding on the outcome. They weren't even playing a game where they could win or lose anything at all. Yet, when a diamond that was supposed to be red actually turned up black, they "freaked out" just like Maria Navarro and the rest of the citizens of Premont did when the 2011–2012 school year began without a football team.

Here's why: Our minds have highly sophisticated systems for making sense of all the things we see and hear and touch and taste every moment of the day. That system works like an automatic assembly line with buckets of assumptions and expectations sitting on either side of a tiny conveyor belt like the kind you might see at a bottling plant or at a car factory. The typical factory has two levels. The ground level is where the assembly line happens. The second floor is where the managers have their offices, overlooking the factory floor.

In your brain, the ground level of the factory is your subconscious, and the second floor houses higher order conscious reasoning functions. The ground floor is where the vast majority of your information processing happens—mostly without you noticing it. Your brain processes tens of thousands of pieces of information every day, most of which you never pay any conscious attention to. And it usually happens flawlessly while the manager (your conscious brain) sits upstairs shuffling paperwork and pondering the mysteries of the universe.

For example, when you hear that an IT manager elected to do something perfectly normal and commonplace like "enhance the security of a website," the sights and sounds of that moment are dumped onto your brain's subconscious assembly line where they move along until your Inner Child (because who else lives in your subconscious?) finds the sense-making bucket labeled "things techie guys do." Your Inner Child then drops that bundle of information in there without much notice and moves on to the next sensory input rolling down the line. When you hear that a corporate manager has "dealt with a troubling employee through direct coaching and performance management techniques" (Manager A), that bundle of information fits neatly into your "management 101" bucket and requires no further attention. Easy peasy. When teachers hear that the superintendent laid off some of the school system's employees, while unpleasant, it is not totally unexpected and so it doesn't get much attention either.

If your conscious brain notices this new information at all, it responds with a resounding "meh," and then moves on to something else more interesting like this week's football game against Valley High or the leftover pizza in the conference

room. This is how your brain processes 99 percent of the
information it receives in a given day.

But what happens when your brain doesn't have a predefined
bucket for some bundle of information that comes rolling down
the assembly line? What happens one day when a computer guy
says he *reduced* the website's security just to make life easier for
customers? What happens when a Texas high school cancels
football? This information doesn't make sense. It doesn't fit
into any bucket, which seriously interferes with your brain's
sorting system. All of a sudden Inner Child hits the emergency
stop button on the sense-making assembly line. Even though
Inner Child has been working overtime in the cavernous
sweatshop of your amygdala for years and years, it is still a
child. And like any child who doesn't know what to do, little
Nicky stops everything and screams "Mommmm!" from the
bottom of the basement steps. All of a sudden, the brain's plant
manager has to stop whatever it's doing to run downstairs and
see what all the fuss is about.

All of a sudden you pay attention.

As one manager in the Decision Pulse study explained to me
in a debrief session, "This is a rigid, highly regulated bureauc-
racy around here and . . . let's face it, [IT people] are usually
linear engineers who care way more about the technology than
the customers. When I saw Sandeep's decision about reducing
the security of the customer portal, it was sort of like 'wait a
second, that's not supposed to happen.'"

In other words: *Mommm!*

When Ernest Singleton suspended sports, it was as if he
showed Premont's students and their teachers a black queen
of diamonds. Only then did the people of Premont alter their
course. Only then were the teachers and students inspired to
change the way education happened.

"The decision to cancel sports, that was the decision, that was
the catalyst that got everything into motion for us," Singleton
said. "It was unbelievable. This one decision got us enough
attention for people to say, 'Maybe we shouldn't let this school

district go down'" (http://www.texasobserver.org/the-writing-on-the-wall/).

What the turnaround at Premont and the Decision Pulse studies show us is that change decisions grab hold of people's attention in a way that change additions never can. But a true change decision also does something else. It provides direction. The Premont decision not only shook people out of their complacency. It also clarified exactly what they were trying to do, and what else would be sacrificed in pursuit of that new direction. Prior to that decision, "saving the school" meant different things to different people in Premont. For some it meant saving the academic institution. But for others it meant saving the football team and the cheerleading squad. Singleton's decision finally clarified exactly what everyone should be working toward.

That's why a single decision can accomplish far more than a series of fiery speeches, bumper stickers, and branding campaigns. Clever slogans and fist pounding might get people's attention, but it won't give people *direction* unless accompanied by a decision.

3
•
Drivers and Passengers
•

PREMONT SCHOOL'S SCRAPE WITH DEATH, AND THEIR miraculous turnaround, is a triumph of change by decision. But for most of those who lived it, it was as much tragedy as it was triumph.

Many students, like Maria Navarro, the freaked-out student body president, valedictorian, and would-be head cheerleader, felt slightly less than triumphant. "It's been horrible," she told reporters. "It's unfair because we have been doing our part. We come to school. We get good grades and yet we are the ones who have to suffer: no football, no homecoming game, no homecoming court. Our senior year, they just took it away from us."

What Maria Navarro was really asking was: *Why did it have to come to this?*

The short answer is: *it didn't.*

If the school administrators and the town leaders had made the necessary decisions in the years leading up to Singleton's fateful judgment, they could have prevented such a drastic decision from the state education association, which may have prevented Ernest Singleton's decision to cancel football in order to save the school.

But they didn't.

That might be the most important lesson of *Domino*. Change decisions shouldn't be used like a fire extinguisher. They shouldn't be kept behind a piece of glass and accessed only in case of emergency. One thing we can count on is that if we choose not to decide, it won't be long before our bosses or investors or legislators or customers will decide for us. By getting into the habit of deciding instead of adding—by making decisions part of your team's standard routine, instead of the leader's tool of last resort—we can inspire enough small adjustments each day to keep us out of the most dire situations in the future.

In the third section of the book, I'm going to show you a framework for incorporating change decisions into your everyday practices. But before we get into that we need to pull over to the side of the road and talk about where your head is at.

Every change decision is a combination of discernment and discipline. Discernment is about knowing the right thing to do. Discipline is about doing the right thing . . . even when it's uncomfortable. The framework you'll read about in the last half of the book is about discernment. The remainder of this chapter is about the mental discipline required to use that framework appropriately.

●

In volatile situations, people can adopt one of two mindsets— that of a driver or that of a passenger. With a driver's mindset, you believe you have the ability to make change happen. With a passenger's mindset, you believe that change is something that happens to you. Drivers believe that the outcome of their life and career is more or less in their own hands, and they wouldn't have it any other way. Passengers take a more Forrest Gump approach to living and working. They sit around and wait for a bus to come by and take them somewhere. Drivers believe that no matter how challenging things might seem or how far things have spun out of control, their decisions still matter, and their actions can still make a difference.

Take a look at the descriptions below and think about how much you think each one describes you. Jot down a number between 1 and 5 next to each statement. The higher the number, the more you agree with the statement, and the lower the number, the less you agree.

1. ___ I am confident I get the success I deserve in life.

2. ___ Sometimes I feel depressed.

3. ___ When I try, I generally succeed.

4. ___ Sometimes when I fail I feel worthless.

5. ___ I complete tasks successfully.

6. ___ Sometimes I do not feel in control of my work.

7. ___ Overall I am satisfied with myself.

8. ___ I am filled with doubts about my competence.

9. ___ I determine what will happen in my life.

10. ___ I do not feel in control of my success in my career.

11. ___ I am capable of coping with most of my problems.

12. ___ There are times when things look pretty bleak and hopeless to me.

Now, add up your scores on the odd-numbered questions. _____

Next, add up your scores on the even-numbered questions. _____

Finally, subtract the even total from the odd total.

Your total score: _____

These 12 questions, created and tested by the psychologist Tim Judge and his colleagues,[1] have been answered by tens of thousands of people all around the world ranging from factory workers on the shop floor and executives in c-suites to expatriates in strange lands, entrepreneurs in the midst of chaotic new ventures, and the newly unemployed in search of more work. Every time the results are the same. People with high scores dramatically outperform people with low scores. They manage their stress better. They adjust better to foreign assignments. They sell more. They deliver better customer service. They look longer and harder for jobs after they've been laid off.

What's the difference?

People with a driver's mindset believe that even if they have to leave behind the stability and safety of the status quo, they will still benefit from decisions that move them forward. They acknowledge the truth about their reality, but then quickly do whatever they can to positively influence that reality. They ask for help. They mobilize others. They step up and continue making decisions to switch lanes here and step on the gas there, even at the risk of making a wrong turn. When they make wrong turns — which they often do because every human being does — they correct their course quickly.

In short, they don't let the pain of loss prevent them from making the right decisions.

People with a passenger's mindset believe their decisions will only make the situation worse. In volatile times, they feel enslaved by their situations. They let their fear of being wrong inhibit their ability to make things right. They pull over and switch on their hazard lights, hoping against hope that somebody else will come along and take the wheel for them. They exert most of their energy ruminating about the unfairness of regulators or bosses or competitors or spouses or acts of God or organizational culture or vindictive family members who put them in this unfavorable situation, instead of strategizing about how to proceed, and then acting on their judgments. Or worse yet, they beat themselves up for the mistakes they made in the past, instead of reminding themselves that they can—even now—still hop into the driver's seat whenever they choose.

Regardless of where you scored on that quick measure of what you believe, the most important thing is what you *do*. If you landed on the driver's side, take a good long look at what you've actually done over the past few weeks and months. Do your actions reflect your empowered beliefs? Have you been thinking like a driver while acting like a passenger? More specifically:

Have you been deciding more than complaining?

Have you spent more time acting boldly, or more time assigning blame?

Have you been asking for feedback, or hiding from criticism?

If you really want to go the extra mile and know the truth, be bold enough to ask those three questions to five or six people you work with, and use those as your baseline for improving over the next three months.

If you landed on the passenger's side of this assessment, then use your score as a wake-up call. When you look back on the big events in your life, I can almost guarantee there were times when you behaved like a driver. You took control and acted confidently. You overcame obstacles and pulled yourself out of sticky situations to accomplish things that seemed iffy at best when you started. But lately, maybe you've dealt with some big changes at work, or you've experienced some setbacks in your personal life like a painful divorce or the illness of a parent or a child. And so maybe you've buried that driver's mindset somewhere in the shadows of your mind. Maybe you used to behave like a driver all the time and now only 20 or 30 percent of the time.

If that's you that's okay.

The truth is that everyone slides back and forth between the driver's and the passenger's mindset, including the most successful people you know today, and the most courageous leaders throughout history. Mahatma Gandhi, Martin Luther King, Harriet Tubman, Mother Theresa, Abraham Lincoln—all had bouts of serious doubt and even full-blown depression. From time to time, they all felt like they weren't up to coping with the changes and challenges facing them. (And if you thought managing an enterprise software upgrade was hard, try abolishing slavery or liberating a nation of 1 billion peasants.) The difference is that they didn't let themselves stay in that passenger's mindset. Even when they *felt* like a passenger, they forced themselves to *behave* like a driver. They stepped up and continued making one decision after another until they achieved their purpose or—in many cases—died trying.

I'm not suggesting you take on a death wish. But I am saying that there is no reason you can't jumpstart a change right now. All it takes is one decision. That's not just a hollow platitude either. The psychologist Shelley Taylor[2] at UCLA has found that the simple act of making a decision shifts our brains into a driver's mindset, even if only temporarily. After making even an inconsequential decision like where to go on vacation, people score more positively on measures of mood. They score higher on feelings of control over their environment, and they feel more optimistic about their future. In other words, they shift their brain into a driver's mindset.

It doesn't even have to be a life-changing decision to start a domino effect in your brain. One of history's great mysteries was the fact that George Washington—in the midst of the most depressing early years of the American Revolution in which his outmanned, underfunded, and poorly trained army was getting clobbered by the vaunted British military—continued sending letters back home specifying minute details for the renovations on his homestead Mount Vernon. Yes, you read that correctly. George Washington was leading a cause that would send him to the hangman's gallows if he failed, and yet he was staying up late at night penning letters that specified what color the curtains should be in the dining room of his house hundreds of miles away.

Was Washington that naïve? Did he underestimate the gravity of his situation? Shelley Taylor's research 200 years later might finally give puzzled historians their answer. These simple decisions that Washington made every night about his home improvement projects kept sliding his mind back over into the driver's seat for the tough decisions he would inevitably have to make in the next day's battles.

It's doubtful that Washington knew exactly what was happening in his brain. What we can be sure of is that his brain was automatically reinforcing this leisurely activity by restoring his mood and his sense of empowerment night after night no matter what happened during the day's gruesome battles.

That's a good lesson for the rest of us as we attempt to execute our own mini-revolutions at work or at home. If you make a decision and leverage that driver's mindset before it vanishes, you can use it to make the next decision easier, and then the one after that, and after that, and so on. Eventually you will find yourself feeling more empowered and more capable more often. If and when you discover that you've slid back into the passenger's seat a few weeks or a few months later, you can start the domino effect once again with another decision. After a while, the driver's mindset will become your brain's default setting.

Every day, whether you lead a team, an organization, a household, or just a life, you will almost certainly have the opportunity and the responsibility to make decisions like the ones you've read about so far. It will scare you to move an "important" project to the back burner for a few months, because when you look at yourself in the mirror, you might not feel like there is an overachiever staring back at you—you might even see one of those lazy losers who really can't "do it all" after all. Those are groundless perceptions.

Oftentimes the fears aren't imagined. They are real. As Sandy found out, leaving some things behind might have negative short-term financial implications. For relationship-oriented leaders, these decisions might create some social awkwardness when you deprioritize projects that you or some of your team members have devoted weeks or months of their blood, sweat, and tears to. You might feel like you're letting them down. They might feel like you are devaluing their contributions to the team. Sometimes, these decisions might even force you to re-evaluate your understanding of what it means to "do the right thing."

I can promise you that the frameworks and techniques you're learning in this book will give you a much simpler way to execute changes faster and more effectively. I still stand by that promise. One hard truth that I can't really sugarcoat is this: Nothing you will read here or anywhere else can change the fact that making change decisions—even relatively small ones—can be an emotionally taxing activity that you will feel visceral urges to avoid and delay. That's why successfully leading change has as much to do with your emotional strength as it does your intellectual capacity.

History teaches us that successful change agents can come in all shapes, sizes, colors, genders, ages, personality types, and IQ levels. The one thing they all have in common—the only thing that distinguishes them from ordinary people—is their willingness to decide when others would not.

But enough about you. Let's move on now to the real source of the problem: *everybody else.*

4

•

The Permission Ceremony, Part 1: The Drama

•

NOT LONG AGO ON A LATE FEBRUARY morning in Nairobi, Jonathan Mburu found himself standing in front of a full hotel ballroom. Jonathan is a slim man in his late forties with wire-rimmed glasses accenting his warm eyes and a confident demeanor. As he stood there that morning dressed in black slacks and a loose-fitting button-down shirt, a grin slowly creeped across his face. The hundreds of eager faces sitting in front of him at round tables of six to seven belonged to managers from the East African division he leads for a multinational communications company.

"I swear," he began while holding a microphone in his left hand, and with his right hand raised like a president being sworn into office.

Today, Jonathan wasn't explicitly promising to uphold his office faithfully. Instead he was publicly giving his team permission to downright ignore many of the projects they deemed most important right up until that day.

"There will be no retribution," he continued over the chuckles slowly erupting from his audience, "for delaying or ignoring any other projects in order to fully devote your focus to stabilizing our technology infrastructure."

I have to confess: 'Twas I who put Mburu up to these theatrics. But I promise you I had a good reason. And Mburu had good reason for playing along with it. Here is the back story.

Eastern Africa had been in the midst of a revolution in digital communications. Thanks to a combination of foreign investment and a rising middle class, the telecom industry had exploded. Not only were the dominant players in the region expanding rapidly, but a slew of new competitors were attempting to siphon off chunks of the market for themselves.

The challenge, as Jonathan explained to me, was that— while they had already defined eight clear priorities—the one thing they must do immediately was stabilize their information technology infrastructure. In the midst of their rapid growth, their technology systems had been patched together into what Jonathan described as a "Frankenstein system." The risk was not only redundant processes that wasted time and resources for the company, but if they weren't careful, the instability could have compromised both the real and perceived quality of their network that their growing customer base increasingly relied on. In the hypercompetitive market, one major slipup could set them back years in terms of brand reputation.

I said, "Okay, great. The first thing I would do is, instead of just listing those priorities as bullet points, you should *rank* them one through eight."

"Yes, I agree. We did that already," Jonathan replied.

"Okay, great," I said. "Is there anything on that list that really sticks out?"

"Yes. No question at all," he said. "Our number one priority is stabilizing the technology infrastructure—nothing else matters if we don't get this done."

"Sounds like you're pretty clear. So, what is the issue?" I asked.

"Well, we are really good at identifying top priorities," Jonathan stated. "Where my team struggles—myself included—is taking *other* things off our plate. Prioritizing isn't our problem. It is deprioritizing that is the challenge."

Once again, he not only had to make a decision that grabbed the department's attention and clearly signaled a turn in the direction of stabilizing the infrastructure and check his mirrors to make sure that everyone was actually following him through the turn.

The question was *how*?

To find out which issues were the true source of the team's problem, we did the unthinkable: We asked them. The results of our survey pointed to two key issues.

●

ISSUE NUMBER ONE: ONE DEPARTMENT, MANY TEAMS

Jonathan's division consisted of six different teams that were divided into sub-teams and sub-sub-teams and sub-sub-sub teams and . . . well, you get the picture. All those teams were lumped together under Jonathan's one pair of watchful eyes. Some of those teams truly did have almost nothing to do with stabilizing the infrastructure, because it simply wasn't part of their job role. So when Jonathan announced "stabilizing the technology infrastructure" was *his* number one priority for the department, roughly half his people nodded politely, and yawned as "blah, blah, blah, stabilize infrastructure, blah, blah, blah" entered their left ear and promptly exited out their right ear.

With seemingly no direct impact on their daily work, why would they truly care?

The rub here is that stabilizing the infrastructure involved a lot more people than the group thought. About 80 percent of the people in the room felt little to no personal responsibility for this objective. It's like voting in a national election—everyone believes voting is vitally important to the democratic process, but most individuals (at least half in every election) don't feel it is important enough to cast their one lonely vote. The general opinion was *I completely understand why this is important for the company and for the department, but I still don't see what it has to do with me and what I do every day.*

From Jonathan's perspective, however, only two of the six teams could honestly say their work had zero impact on stabilizing the infrastructure. That was what made Jonathan nervous. Some teams had to define the business processes performed by each of the disparate technology systems. Others had to make sure the old systems could talk to the new systems. Still others had to make sure all the employees scattered throughout the region were sufficiently trained on how to use any new systems. One of the team leaders had to pull some of his utility players off of other projects in order to enable them to help out the teams who were devoted solely to the stabilizing project. That of course left a vacancy on the other project teams from which they had just been pulled. In other words, everyone in the department would and should feel some kind of a ripple effect if a shift in focus actually occurred.

But even still, many of the people in the department were not directly related to the IT systems. To address this issue, Jonathan sat down with his five direct reports prior to the two-day meeting that morning in Nairobi and identified two other initiatives from their list of 10—number 3: upgrade customer payment solutions and number 9: make usage data consistent across customer groups.

Now, every single team leader in the department—from supervisor to senior vice president—could see a direct link

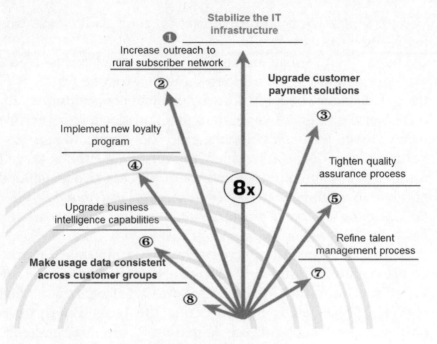

Figure 4.1   Pulse Tree

between their work and at least one critical departmental priority.

●

ISSUE NUMBER TWO: "IT'S TAKING THINGS OFF OUR PLATE THAT'S OUR PROBLEM"

Even more important for the success of their strategic shift was that now every team member could identify which projects were acceptable to deprioritize. As Jonathan had predicted, that was the real challenge all along. After all, it wasn't like the Mburu Team had just been sitting around twiddling their thumbs until one day the IT infrastructure project suddenly landed in their collective lap. All 300 of them had big, busy, full-plate jobs long before this project was even a sparkle in their fearless leaders' eyes. Those other priorities, ongoing initiatives, and cross-functional project teams didn't magically disappear now that stabilizing the infrastructure—important as it was—had been ratcheted up to top priority.

Jonathan and his leadership team had fired the first shot with the ranked list of priorities—and naming one top priority that every team member's work could be linked directly to. Everyone could now look at whichever of those top three priorities fit their function, and then prioritize accordingly. For example, if you had some connection to either the back-end technology or the front-end business process that depended on the technology systems, you now knew that all your projects relating to the stabilization of the infrastructure deserved more of your attention than those related to the loyalty program or the refining of talent management. And if you had no connection to the stabilization of the infra-structure, then you knew that all your projects related to upgrading customer payment solutions would be higher pri-ority than those related to upgrading business intelligence solutions or to those that would contribute to tightening quality assurance processes.

Perhaps most importantly, the team had to know that it was not just *okay*, but that it was actually *expected* that they would spend less time and effort contributing to the lower priority projects. That was the hard part.

As another employee explained it to me once, Jonathan said, "People here wear their busyness like a badge of honor." Our surveys reveal that nearly 60 to 65 percent of managers from a cross section of industries and organizations believe they would actually *lose* respect from their peers and their bosses if they focused on their top priorities at the expense of other lower-ranked priorities. This means that even if people fully under-stand their individual roles in stabilizing the infrastructure, and fully understand what else they should put on the shelf for a little while, they feel silently pressured by their company culture—their bosses, their peers, and even their team members to just soldier on anyway, and to continue being productive on anything and everything no matter how much the focus of the business unit has shifted.

My research and experience has led me to conclude that this feeling is almost universal. In almost every organization I've worked with or studied, there is an unspoken but widely held fear of retribution. People naturally assume that they will be subtly, if not explicitly, punished for ignoring the projects that had just been clearly deprioritized. Believe it or not, our surveys have shown that most managers believe they would be more effective leaders if they increased their focus on just a few initiatives by abandoning other initiatives, they also believe that this decision to focus will lose them respect.

Think about it: In most organizations, managers derive a lot of their worth from being known as the kind of person that "gets things done." It's only natural then to feel like people would think less of you if you abandoned some of those projects instead of "getting 'er done." If they asked you to help out with implementing the new loyalty program and you said, "Gee, I wish I could but I've got these other priorities I'm married to . . . ," there is a fear that you might be seen as lazy or unhelpful. Worse yet it might even earn you some "performance coaching."

That's how Jonathan came to be standing in front of his department with his right hand in the air, repeating the words, "I swear . . . that if you focus on stabilizing the infrastructure, even if it means not working on the other projects on this list or any other priorities, there will be no retribution or punishment of any kind."

The permission ceremony grabbed their attention and clearly pointed to the new direction. He had signaled the turn in a way that spoke to each manager in his department. The question now is whether they actually intended to make the turn with him.

SECTION 2

•

Check Your Mirrors

•

5

•

The Permission Ceremony, Part 2: The Conflict

•

WHEN YOU HAVE SOMEONE FOLLOWING YOU IN a car, how do you know if they noticed your turn signal? How do you know whether or not they intend to follow you around the turn?

Your best bet is to look in the rearview mirror and verify that they also switched on their blinker. When you're leading a team, you can do the same thing—sort of. Problem is that your people probably don't come to work every morning wearing little light bulbs sheathed under orange reflectors on their shoulders (or at least not when OSHA pays a visit). In the absence of that literal blinking light, you need another clear indicator of your team members' intentions to get out of the old lane and follow you into the new lane.

That was Jonathan's challenge.

His oath was kind of funny, kind of strange, and awfully effective at signaling his turn. But it wasn't yet clear that everyone was following him. He still needed to see their blinkers in his rearview mirror.

So after Jonathan finished his oath, we split the room up into the five major sub-teams. Each team was tasked with two objectives.

First, they created a 90-day sprint that identified the top three objectives they would commit to focusing on for the next 90 days.

Second, they created a waitlist with all the other objectives for the year that they would intentionally put on hold for 90 days or until their three sprint objectives were completed.

When they were finished, each team had a document that looked like this:

OUR TEAM PULSE: Stabilize the IT Infrastructure

90-DAY SPRINT

1. Stabilize the infrastructure by documenting key customer touchpoints

2. Fine-tune customer data protection protocols

3. Implement experiential marketing campaign in coastal region

90-DAY WAITLIST

4. Increase size of enterprise solution branding team

5. Finish market research on urban customer usage patterns

6. Expand business service facilities

7. Digitize new product training materials

Figure 5.1   Mburu Sprint Waitlist

At that point, the permission ceremony continued. So after each of his direct reports finished their sprints and waitlists, I brought the microphone over to Cynthia, one of the members of Jonathan's leadership team. Looking at her team members assembled right in front of her, and visible to the entire department, she said, "I swear there will be no retribution for putting other priorities on the back burner until our team's top three priorities are completed." From Cynthia, the mike traveled to Noney, who repeated the same oath. Noney was followed by Austin, then Mike, then Carol, and then Susan.

One by one, each of the six members of the department's leadership team switched on their blinkers for the rest of the department to see.

That's also when the road rage set in.

Susan was the last of Jonathan's direct reports to give her team permission to hold off on their defined waitlist. All seemed to be going well right up until she announced that "implement new loyalty program" was on her waitlist. She was the third of the five team leaders to relegate the loyalty program to her team's waitlist.

At that point, the fecal matter hit the fan.

Susan's peer, Cynthia, and her team were directly responsible for the loyalty program in the larger organization. For at least eight of the managers on Cynthia's team, the loyalty program was almost 100 percent of their job, and it had been for years. Before today, they had been told that their job was vitally important, not just to Cynthia's team, but to the entire organization. And now, it seemed as though half of the department— their trusted colleagues and friends—were announcing to a ballroom full of confidantes that their baby was ugly.

Not surprisingly, this upset the loyalty program team. I don't mean that chairs started flying or that the meeting suddenly erupted into a Jerry Springer episode. But the loyalty program team's discontent was obvious. In a delicious little irony, the loyalty program team felt that their peers were being viciously disloyal.

When you think about it, wouldn't you be a little perturbed too? What if half the people in your organization suddenly said, "Hey, you know that thing you do—that thing you've spent the past 18 months working overtime on, coming dangerously close to an imbalanced work-life relationship. Yeah . . . uh, that doesn't really matter to us. So we're gonna 86 it for a while." How would that make *you* feel?

Typically, we chalk this up to the notorious problems of siloes and turf wars and an unwillingness to collaborate. But I'm not sure if that's it. It is simply human nature to feel bad when everybody seems to be ganging up on you, and when they devalue something that you highly value. It's natural to feel personally degraded and professionally frustrated.

At this point in our show one sing-songy word was running through everyone's mind: *Awkwarrrddd.*

I wish I could say that this was an isolated occurrence. But that would be a bold-faced lie. This awkwardness happens on cue, virtually every time I get to this part of a workshop. Invariably, some team's top priorities will wind up on another team's waitlist. When that knowledge is made public, things get uncomfortable. Not long ago, this exact scenario played out in a different organization. Only this time, the priority that got waitlisted belonged to the team led by the person who hired me. Their top priority was employee engagement, which was one of the organization's top four priorities overall. However, when the COO announced her team's 90-day waitlist, guess what was right there at the top? Yep—*employee engagement.* Oops. Talk about biting the hand that feeds you.

So why do I continue making teams do this exercise that makes the room so uncomfortable, and threatens my relationship with client contacts? Am I a sadist? Do I just like to see people squirm? Not at all. In fact, I'm nonconfrontational to a fault. My fragile ego really doesn't like to be the object of other people's scorn. So am I just dumb? Or am I really that bad at business development that I intentionally ostracize the people who are probably going to be signing my checks? Probably. But that's not why I do it.

Consider the alternative for Jonathan's team. Each of Jonathan's teams defines their 90-day priorities and their wait-lists, but in order to avoid the awkwardness, they don't announce them to the rest of the department. In this scenario, everyone leaves the workshop feeling inspired, focused, and just positively chipper. They fly back home energized and ready to dig into their top priorities.

But then three days later someone from Cynthia's loyalty program team calls up someone from Susan's team and the conversation goes like this:

"Hey, friend, wasn't that a fun meeting last week?"

"Yep. Except for that clown Nick, everything else was great!"

"Yes, definitely. Anyway, I was just wondering when you think you'll be able to get that stuff to me you were working on for the loyalty program initiative?"

"Oh, yeah . . . that. Uh, well, you see . . . Susan said that, um. . . . Er, that's actually on my waitlist now."

"Huh? What do you mean? Cynthia said it's my number one priority?"

"Uhhh. . . ."

Whoops.

At this point, both people are confused and starting to get frustrated. Neither of them knows what to do. So one of two things will happen next.

If it's a highly collaborative culture, or the person from Susan's team is just a really nice person, he will disregard the top objectives on his own team's sprint and waitlist and say, "Okay, I'll get it to you by the end of the week. Will that work?" Never mind his own top priorities that he just signed off on a week before.

If, however, he is a confrontational person, he might instead say, "Sorry, bub, no can do. Orders are orders. You're just gonna have to wait. I know that the loyalty program is *your* top priority, but I'm afraid that also makes it *your* problem." This time he has held his ground and remained focused. But in the process he has burnt a bridge and stifled the collaborative culture the organization has worked so hard to foster.

Neither scenario is especially good. So what is the alternative?

Answer: Address it head on, team leader to team leader, right then and there in the meeting.

Because we address this publicly at the workshop with all the teams and leaders in the room together, the leaders can get out in front of the inevitable conflicts that will happen with their team members down the road. To stave off bloodshed, however, I always reiterate that this is only a *90-day* waitlist, and not a *lifetime* waitlist. In other words, it's only on the waitlist temporarily. So just because three of the five teams put the loyalty program on their waitlist for the next 90 days doesn't mean that the loyalty program won't be a top priority for all of them in the next 90 days.

Second, it doesn't even mean that the loyalty program is somehow less important to the department, or that this area isn't valued. In fact, what it meant in this case is that the loyalty program team had been doing their job so effectively in recent months that the loyalty program initiative didn't require special attention. Instead of being an insult, it was actually a compliment. The loyalty program—unlike the IT infrastructure—was already pretty effective, so it didn't need urgent attention.

Third, it didn't mean that the whole department should completely ignore the loyalty program. It just meant that the loyalty program was in a kind of temporary *maintenance* mode rather than *improvement* mode. It's like the loyalty program was in a job-sharing situation after coming back from paternity leave. Oftentimes people misinterpret the waitlist to mean that they are agreeing to let these projects slip into complete disrepair for the next 90 days. Understandably they object to this. But that's not what the waitlist means at all. It just means you aren't going to actively devote extra resources to improving the waitlist items—which is very different from saying you are going to let it get *worse*.

By publicly announcing each team's waitlists, Jonathan's leaders could make it clear that the waitlist is not a "blacklist," and explain the thinking behind each of the waitlist items. Susan and Cynthia were able to lead by example and show their team members how it would look to constructively work through conflicting priorities with another team. On top of that, Jonathan was able to visibly check whether each of his direct reports had in fact signaled their intention to switch lanes. By the end of the Nairobi meeting, he was confident each of his top leaders clearly understood how the department's new priorities fit together, and how they were expected to put other things on hold in order to pursue them.

In the other organization where "employee engagement" was waitlisted by the COO, sharing the waitlist with the team helped her and the head of HR lead by example. The COO was able to explain that she put employee engagement on her waitlist not because she didn't think it was important. On the contrary, she felt it was *so important* to her team that she had already put a process in place weeks before that meeting in order to boost her team's engagement. So over the next 90 days she didn't need to devote additional creative resources to figuring out how to boost engagement—she simply needed to maintain the efforts she had already begun.

In turn, the HR director was able to further focus his team's pursuit of their top priority. Now instead of spending the next 90 days trying to boost staff engagement equally all across the organization, he decided to narrow his team's focus. By really digging into the engagement issues of only a few departments at a time every 90 days, they were able to apply more customized solutions that addressed the specific issues of each department rather than applying general and largely superficial engagement solutions to every department.

6

•

Who's That Behind You?

•

I HAVE A CONFESSION TO MAKE: I am kind of a stalker.

This is to say that I have a mild obsession with watching people in the act of deciding. Some people call this sort of thing "research." But the truth is that I collect decisions like John Hinckley collected Jodi Foster photos. I even set up a company called Decision Pulse in order to formalize my voyeuristic pursuits. At Decision Pulse, we collect big decisions and little decisions. We collect decisions made by clients ranging from corporate executives, middle managers, and entrepreneurs as well as decisions made by famous people, such as rock stars, celebrity chefs, and sports figures. We even collect decisions from almost perfect strangers who graciously offer up their choices on our website in exchange for helpful feedback about their natural decision styles. This last group consists of people like college students, teachers, stay-at-home moms and dads, and people like your reclusive neighbor down the block who seems strangely fascinated with taxidermy.

In the past few years, we've compiled roughly 143,000 decisions in our not-so-cleverly named "Decision Database." We keep them in a database because our surveys show that people think a database is substantially less creepy than plastering the decisions of perfect strangers on my bedroom wall. My wife agrees.

Whether you choose to call what we do "stalking," "research," or "Google's business model," the fact is that I have spent a disturbing number of hours every day for the past decade swimming around in a big, steaming pile of other people's decisions. As a result, we've learned quite a bit about how people make decisions and why some decisions impact people in ways that other decisions don't. We've also learned quite a lot about the people who make those decisions. One of the most startling conclusions we've reached is this:

People. Are. Different.

Who knew, right?

This means that the way you make decisions might be very different from the way some of the people on your team make decisions, while others you're very similar to and still others are somewhere in between. When you're trying to inspire this collection of individuals to follow you and continue following you all the way through the change, it's helpful to have some idea about how each of these individual *persons* tend to drive.

I think of this as the Ron versus Rod Distinction. For example, when I have my father, Ron Tasler, following me on the road, I know I have to drive very differently from how I have to drive if I have my father-in-law, Rod Lieske, following me on the road. Ron Tasler's driving style is shaped by unspoken guidelines such as *yellow lights are cues to speed up*; *turn signals are totally optional*; and *tailgating is just how you establish an intimate personal connection with your fellow drivers.*

Rod Lieske, a former driver's education instructor, has a style shaped by a very different set of guidelines. He will always be precisely two-and-a-half car lengths behind you; he never goes a single digit higher than the speed limit; and yellow lights are treated as an opportunity to slow down and collect your thoughts.

So when I come to a stoplight with Ron Tasler in tow, I know that yellow means not just "go," but "go *fast*" . . . or I'm likely to get rear-ended. I know that he too wants to make it through the yellow light, and I also know that his vehicle will never be more than six inches behind my rear bumper the entire trip. (In fairness to my dad—as he is always quick to remind me—he hasn't had so much as a fender bender in over 40 years. *Touché*, Dad. *Touché*.)

When I come to an intersection with Rod Lieske following me, even if I'm approaching a green light I know that I'd better slow down a little just in case the green light turns yellow, because yellow means "stop" if I want to arrive at our destination with the full caravan intact.

As a student of psychology, what I find most fascinating about the Ron versus Rod phenomenon is that these two men were born within a year of each other. Both have primarily German ancestry. Both were raised in the same era in middle-class households in rural farming communities in the upper Midwest region of the United States. And yet, their approaches to driving (not to mention investing, working, parenting, and living) could hardly be further apart.

What's the point, you ask?

People. Are. Different.

That means that simple demographic breakdowns (also known as stereotypes)—age, gender, marital status, ethnicity, sexual preference, education—within your team or your organization aren't going to tell you nearly enough of what you need to know about how different team members are likely to make change decisions. Overly simplistic distinctions won't tell you how some of your team members' approaches to change decisions will differ in relation to yours and to their other teammates.

However, at the risk of sounding like a self-serving hypocrite (I've been called much worse) we can still make meaningful distinctions between people in terms of the way they approach decisions. But instead of using demographics, we can still classify individuals by their behavior patterns or "decision styles." The reason why decision styles make sense where demographic distinctions don't is because these decision styles describe our conscious choices. We can't choose our ancestry. We can't choose when we were born. We can't choose where we were born. We can't choose how we were raised, or who our parents were. All of these historical variables certainly play a role in shaping our decision styles, but they say nothing about how each of us has chosen to respond to our demographic origins. More specifically, these generalizations tell us almost nothing about how your people will likely view the kinds of situations your plan is going to put them into. Which variables in each decision situation will they pay the most attention to, and which pieces of the puzzle are they likely to ignore?

For instance, most people—between 69 percent and 75 percent—tend to be more cautious and risk averse.[1] When given a choice between two options, they are two to three times more likely to prefer the guaranteed, no-risk, bird-in-the-hand option rather than chase the more uncertain prospect of two birds in the bush. That's because, on average, these people pay almost three times more attention to what they might *lose* in a potential change situation than what they might gain from that exact same situation.

But that's not the whole story. A solid minority of people (25 to 30 percent) is drawn more to potential opportunity than they are to possible risks. When given the choice between accepting a guarantee of earning $1,000 or a fifty-fifty chance of winning $2,000, they will typically select the gamble. That's because they focus more on the size of the reward than they do the probability of actually obtaining that award.

The differences between those two groups is magnified during times of proposed change when emotions run high and logic runs . . . uh, let's just say "less high." The better you understand the styles of the people you're working with, the simpler it will be to inspire the right people to make the right changes.

That was the epiphany that led to Fabrizio Freda's turn-around of Estee Lauder a few years ago.[2] In 2008, Freda became the first person outside of the Lauder family bloodline to take the helm of Estee Lauder. His top priority was getting the company's brand managers to give up their obsession with growing sales, and instead to focus on increasing profits. Just as conventional wisdom tells us, the managers were none too happy with the proposed change. After all, every corporate veteran knows that "increase profits" is just politically correct shorthand for "slash your spending a.s.a.p." And what could be less *fun* than cutting spending?

Lauder's brand managers—most of whom cut their teeth in sales and marketing—had conditioned themselves to think like reward seekers, rather than cost managers. For them, growing sales was interesting and exciting work. But trying to expand profit margins? Not so much. In their eyes that was boring, bean-counter work. Best to leave that for the accountants. Freda recognized that distinction and used it to his advantage.

Jane Lauder, the ranking family member at Estee Lauder, explained that Freda's real stroke of genius—why he succeeded where his predecessors had failed—was in getting the brand managers to focus on the gain rather than the loss. "Your eyes glaze over," Lauder told *Fortune* magazine, "when you hear about return on equity . . . but you have a real appreciation if you can spend those savings on things that really drive sales."

Freda recognized that his brand managers were not part of that cautious majority. This group wouldn't be motivated by propaganda about how this new plan would mitigate future risk or help stabilize their earnings. They wanted growth, not stability. That's why the "burning platform" shtick—which can be quite effective with many people—just doesn't do a whole lot for reward seekers.

"[Brand managers] were afraid they wouldn't grow," Freda explained. "I showed that they could keep growing and make a lot more money if they cut expenses and plowed the money back into what was *profitable*, not just *growing*." He got the attention of his reward-seeking brand managers by deciding to suspend the focus on growth. Yes, ultimately he wanted growth too. But he knew that growth might have to be temporarily sacrificed on the altar of their future success, in order to get the organization refocused on profit. He explained how this new focus on profit would actually *increase* their ability to grow sales and to stake their claim on even more rewards.

And he was right. In the first four years of the plan, sales grew by 40 percent, while costs had increased by only 8 percent.

After all that, I bet you're dying to know what your decision style is, aren't you? To find out, go to www.decisionpulse.com. When you're finished meet me at the start of the next chapter.

7

•

How to Be a Stalker

•

HOW DO THE PEOPLE ON YOUR TEAM view most situations? What do they focus on when they make decisions? For that matter, which variables of the situation do you focus on when you make a decision? How long is the time horizon you typically consider when making decisions? When you make a decision, do you value speed more than thoroughness and prudence? Or is it the other way around for you?

Thanks to my extensive experience with stalking, you can learn the answers to these questions. And with a little luck and a lot of hard work, maybe someday you too can be a stalker.

To begin, we find it most helpful to understand people's decision tendencies along three dimensions.

1. **Operational versus Conceptual:** Do you tend to approach strategic decisions more operationally or conceptually?

2. **Risky versus Cautious:** Are you drawn more to high-risk/high-reward options, or do you view your options from a more cautious perspective?

3. **Deliberative versus Impulsive:** Do you like to make sure you have all the facts before deciding, or do you just get on with it?

Understanding where you land on each of these three continuums can tell you a lot about the way you like to approach changes and how you like to go about executing plans. Are you constantly looking at the big picture, or do you get charged up by digging into the details and really getting your hands dirty? Just as importantly, you can also learn a lot about the way the people on your team approach change and execution. In which situations are they likely to thrive? Where are the blind spots and stumbling blocks most likely to appear?

When you put these three dimensions together you wind up with one of eight general profiles or "styles." (The eight styles are listed below.) The collective style of the group can tell us quite a bit about the culture of execution on that team or within that organization.

We recently helped the managers at a regional healthcare provider bridge the gap between their new strategy and the execution of that strategy. The executive team felt some trepidation about how quickly and effectively the organization would be able to deploy this strategy. In our diagnostic survey, we saw that the managers were remarkably clear about the top priorities of the organization in this new plan. However, they were deeply concerned that too many urgencies would arise throughout the day that would distract them from focusing on those top priorities.

The group's decision style illuminated the source of this challenge. Their management ranks were dominated by Builders—people who are operational, cautious, and deliberative.

Builders are great at digging into the details of a situation, and they really don't like leaving things to chance whenever they can help it. Their mantra is *better to be safe and diligent, rather than sorry and broke.* While those tendencies are highly effective for managers in times of stability, Builders can easily feel overwhelmed in times of change and uncertainty—when the old "building" is getting remodeled or torn down before it has even been completed. They don't like loose ends and they hate leaving things partially completed even when those things are no longer a priority. This group felt overwhelmed by the volume of urgent issues they faced every day because they felt like doing their job effectively required them to respond immediately and diligently to every hiccup and fire drill that came across their desk or dropped into their inbox. That told us that in order to help this group, first and foremost we needed to help them redefine what "urgent" actually meant, and then reclassify which issues, and their priorities in the job right now, were actually urgent and which fires they needed to let burn while dealing with other issues.

Another issue is that those leaders in the executive ranks were mostly Hunters and Inventors—people who tend to think more conceptually and are less risk averse. Even though all the layers of management seemed perfectly clear about what the strategic priorities were, there was a notable gap in the way that the executives expected the strategy to be executed and the way in which the lower level mangers actually approached execution.

Neither of these issues is especially rare, and both of them are eminently solvable. Our studies show that the only demographic variable that can reasonably predict decision styles is job title. The higher up you go in an organization the more likely people are to be conceptual versus operational. We haven't tracked it over time for a long enough period to determine conclusively whether job title is the chicken or the egg—whether conceptual thinkers are more likely to be promoted, or whether people who get promoted started out thinking more conceptually. Our hypothesis is that it's a little bit of both, but what related research shows is leading us to believe that it is probably more of the latter.

Either way, the gap in styles between lower and upper levels of management is fairly common. The important thing is that you are aware of whether that gap exists for you and your team, so you can make your styles work for you instead of against you.

If you missed it in Chapter 6, you and your team members can find your decision styles for free at www.decisionpulse.com. If you are digitally deprived at the moment, the information on the following pages will give you a pretty good idea about which decision style belongs to you. For extra credit, you can guess which style your team members belong to also.

Table 7.1   Know

Results	KNOW	
	Operational	**Conceptual**
Highly Operational	Decision makers with this score are very operational in their approach to decisions. They enjoy digging into operational details and being as productive as possible on whatever assignment happens to come their way. Sometimes their preference for efficiency causes them to pay too little attention to the broader vision and strategy of the organization and to overlook big picture opportunities and threats.	
Moderately Operational	Decision makers in this range tend to think more often about near-term tactics than long-term strategy. They prefer to focus their energy on translating strategic priorities into actionable steps, and on completing each project with maximum efficiency. They place a higher emphasis on performing operational duties well, rather than discussing future possibilities.	

Moderately Conceptual	Decision makers in this range tend to think conceptually more often than not. They are interested in connecting the dots between overarching strategic priorities and current issues and projects facing their team. They like discussing future opportunities, but can become impatient and frustrated when required to manage tactical details.
Highly Conceptual	Decision makers with this score tend to think very conceptually—focusing on the big picture implications for every situation. They prefer to think often about the role they play in the overall strategy. They sometimes spend too much time analyzing the future while paying too little attention to the tasks of today.

Table 7.2 Think

Results	THINK	
	Risky	**Cautious**
Highly Risky	Decision makers in this score range tend to pursue high reward opportunities even if it means exposing themselves to substantial risk. They pay special attention to opportunity costs, rather than dwelling on the obvious risks. They strongly believe that taking risks is essential to success. While that belief can sometimes enable them to explore opportunities that others shy away from, it can also cause them to downplay serious threats.	

(continued)

Table 7.2   (*Continued*)

Results	THINK	
	Risky	**Cautious**
Moderately Risky	Decision makers in this range tend to be riskier than normal. New opportunities excite them at least as much they scare them. When making team decisions they might lean toward safer choices when possible, but their first instinct usually favors the bolder, higher reward option even if it comes with higher risk.	
Moderately Cautious	Decision makers in this range are moderately cautious. They feel most comfortable steering clear of risks, and pride themselves on being prudent decision makers. They will pursue appealing opportunities when possible, but they like to be certain that the chance of a good outcome greatly outweighs the risks of a bad outcome.	
Highly Cautious	Decision makers in this score range tend to be very careful decision makers. They rarely support high-risk pursuits and do not like to expose themselves to uncontrollable circumstances. Their role in team decisions is not to prevent risk-taking, instead making sure there is a Plan B in case the risky move fails to pay off.	

Table 7.3 Do

Results	DO	
	Deliberative	**Impulsive**
Highly Impulsive	Decision makers in this score range are very impulsive. They usually put a premium on the speed of action and tend to be more comfortable figuring things out as they go rather than taking a wait-and-see approach. A high doer's penchant for decisive action can be a tremendous asset to their personal and team success. However, decision quality can suffer when "decisiveness" becomes an excuse for impatience or laziness.	
Moderately Impulsive	Decision makers in this range tend to be impulsive. They prefer not to waste time with what they perceive as endless debate, and they often carry a bias toward action. They typically have some respect for the process of deliberation. But they most often believe that decisions simply need to be made even when there is no clear right answer or when there is no apparent option available that pleases everyone.	
Moderately Deliberative	Decision makers in this range tend to be more deliberative. They like to analyze decisions thoroughly and ensure that they have all of the relevant data necessary before committing to a course of action. They typically enjoy the act of thinking, and don't mind withholding judgment until they've had a chance to dig deep into a situation and uncovered all of the contributing variables.	

(continued)

Table 7.3 (*Continued*)

Results	DO	
	Deliberative	**Impulsive**
Highly Deliberative	Decision makers in this range are very deliberative. They are not bothered by complex problems and usually enjoy the act of thinking through a problem and the possible scenarios as much as they enjoy arriving at the solution. They tend to pursue ideal solutions for the sake of ideal solutions. When taken to extremes, this tendency can sometimes lead to analysis paralysis and stunt progress.	

PART TWO

•

Adapt to Change

•

SECTION I

•

Anticipate

•

8

•

Seriously, Who Keeps Moving My Cheese?!?

•

HERE'S THE DIRTY LITTLE SECRET WE DON'T read about often enough in business books. You know all of those success stories you just read about? The ones where gritty teams who applied the tools and techniques that I, the sagely author, have come just short of promising will guarantee you fame, fortune, eternal purpose, and the realization of all your wildest dreams?

That's not exactly the whole story. When we read a neat and tidy summary of how this plucky manager or that well-oiled team beat the odds and sailed smoothly to victory thanks to one or two good decisions and deep devotion to a 90-day sprint and waitlist, it implies that "change" is an orderly, predictable annual or quarterly occurrence. We see a change on the

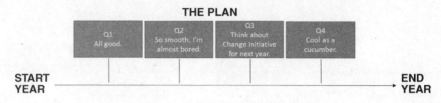

Figure 8.1   The Plan

horizon. We develop a plan to inspire the necessary changes in our people. We kick off the plan. We revisit it every quarter to make touch-ups around the edges. Then at the end of the year—because change of course is constant—we start working on another plan. Schematically, that idyllic fantasy looks something like Figure 8.1.

Problem is that change is like breathing. Neither one is a project that can be managed to completion.

In reality, every single one of the heroic teams in those earlier stories had to do a complete reevaluation of priorities within three months of making their initial change decision. For some teams, their priorities shifted a little. For others, they shifted a lot. In one case, a long-awaited go-ahead decision from the corporate headquarters came through on a highly fruitful project no more than a month after we hatched their big new change plan. Time for another change decision.

In another case, the manager most directly responsible for the new direction—a rising star in the company—couldn't handle the spotlight role. Time for another change decision. The division president had to reassign him elsewhere in the company barely halfway through that first 90-day sprint.

For a different group, the correct change decision came too little too late. Just three weeks later the group was decimated by layoffs. Time's up. No time for another change decision.

In a happier case, the mother company landed a strategic alliance that filled the hole this department's entire change effort was intended to plug—project complete. Time for a different change.

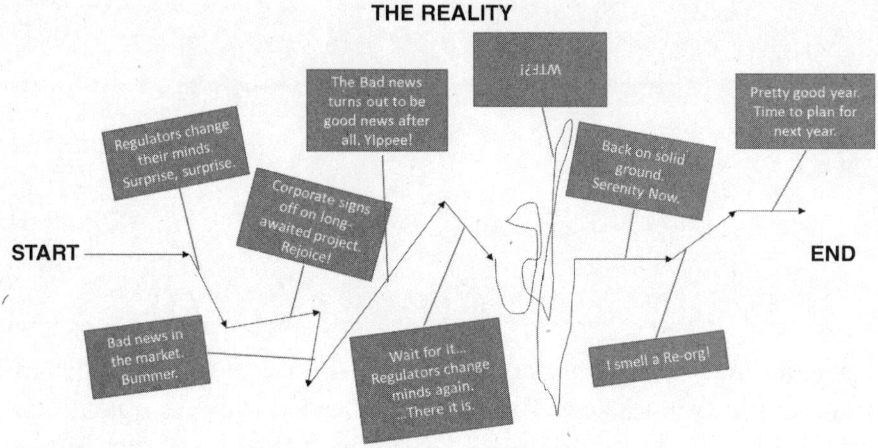

THE REALITY

The Bad news turns out to be good news after all. Yippee!

WTF?!

Pretty good year. Time to plan for next year.

Regulators change their minds. Surprise, surprise.

Back on solid ground. Serenity Now.

Corporate signs off on long-awaited project. Rejoice!

START

END

Bad news in the market. Bummer.

Wait for it... Regulators change minds again. ...There it is.

I smell a Re-org!

Figure 8.2   The Reality

Most often, the changes were small and ambiguous. In the case of one pharmaceutical company charged with complying with a strict new federal regulation, the urgent change project dragged on for more than a year as the federal regulators kept changing the definition of "compliant."

In real life, these neat stories look more like Figure 8.2.

Twenty years ago, leaders all over the world were trying to figure out "who moved my cheese?"[1] Today, they're trying to make peace with the fact that their cheese never stops moving. So in the second half of this book, we're going to zoom out. We're going to look at how to use the basic insights from Part I about inspiring a single change, in order to manage the everyday job of leading in a world that stubbornly refuses to stop changing every few weeks or months.

The question is *how*?

9

Pivots and Power Strokes

IMAGINE CANOEING DOWN A BUBBLING BROOK WITH a couple of pals. The fresh autumn breeze soothes your throat and cools your face. You quietly take in the sights of freshly fallen leaves painting the riverbanks in stunning shades of orange, red, and yellow.

Then suddenly you float around a bend and spot a fork in the river. The right branch of the fork leads to another tranquil stretch of stream. But that's not where you're headed. You are drifting toward the left fork. Your pupils balloon as you watch the river's powerful current thrust you ever closer to a swirling, foaming, Class 5 rapids.

What do you do?

The instinctive reaction is to start making what are called "power strokes" on the left side of the boat, which is basically just river-rafting jargon for paddling like your life (or at least your *dryness*) depends on it. Thanks to your frenzied power stroking on the left side of the boat, your wobbly vessel mercifully begins to angle toward the right.

But it is a painfully long and wide arc of a turn. Those power strokes are a catch-22. The harder and more forcefully you paddle to make the turn in time, the faster you hurl your boat downstream closer and closer to the dangerous fork ahead. At this point, you are doing as much praying as you are paddling, and then. . . .

Whoa. That was close. You made it just before things got ugly.

But the trip is far from over. And now you know that this river has some gnarly sets of rapids, and the one you just avoided will not be the last. Your anxious thoughts kick into overdrive. You wonder how confident you'll feel when you see the next rocky cluster a few hundred meters downstream. You start suspiciously eyeing your boatmates, wondering how committed they really are to seeing this thing through until the end. You think to yourself *how exhausted are we all going to feel after power stroking our way through every twist and turn? How long before someone falls overboard? How long before the boat capsizes? How tense is the rest of this trip going to be with everyone white-knuckling the oars while we drift helplessly along under the long shadow of impending doom?*

Your exciting adventure has just become a case study in group dynamics under stress, uncertainty, and exhaustion.

But now imagine a different technique. When you see the split—rapids on the left, smooth sailing on the right—the people in the front dig their paddles in, and pull the water behind them as hard as they can. But this time, the person sitting in the back doesn't power stroke with them. The back person drops their oar into the water on the opposite side of the boat, and begins to pry the oar away from the boat. With those motions working together—power stroking up front and prying away from the boat in the back, the canoe suddenly pivots as if it's anchored to an invisible hinge on the river bottom.

The canoe's nose turns right while the tail slides left. It doesn't make a long arc or a wide curve like it does with only the power strokes. It simply swivels to the right without propelling you any further downstream.

The pivot turn accomplishes the same change in direction as all-out power stroking. But it does so far more swiftly and efficiently. It doesn't waste excess energy and it leaves your crew with plenty of time to spare before you reach the rocky rapids ahead. Perhaps the greatest advantage of pivot turns is that everyone in the boat now feels confident in their ability to quickly maneuver their way past the next set of rapids or rocky shoreline or random piece of debris in the waters ahead.

The same journey that was once a fight for survival has become the engaging adventure you hoped it would be.

Leading a team is like that.

●

But you don't work in a canoe, do you? Yeah, me neither. I guess if you work in healthcare or financial services, you probably know something about what it feels like to paddle your way down a shifty river in a semi-steady watercraft with unexpected twists and turns and obstacles around every bend, don't you?

Come to think of it, educators and administrators in school systems like the one in Premont, Texas probably know a thing or two about that feeling as well. Of course if you work in retail or manufacturing, you're probably no stranger to turbulent sales cycles and unplanned detours either. Round and round e-commerce goes, where the next evolution will go, nobody knows.

And speaking of all things e-related, I guess folks in the tech sector could use their supercharged imaginations to imagine what it's like for our boaters, too—knowing that you are always just one disruptive innovation away from overnight immortality or instant obsolescence.

Or what about industry captains in energy taking wild guesses about the future of fossil fuels, climate change, solar power, wind farms, and geopolitics?

How about the movers and shakers of the media and entertainment world who are trying to stay on top of downloading
technology and monopoly-prone distributors?

On second thought, maybe land-lubbin' leaders like you and
me can learn as much from the physics of canoeing as we can
from the details of driving. After spending the last decade and
a half rubbing elbows with teams and leaders in all these
industries, I have yet to meet a single one who looks to the
future and says, "Ya know what? I think we're good. We're just
gonna chillax for the next five years or so."

On one hand, sometimes we have no choice but to power
stroke our way forward. When faced with the need to change
rapidly and frequently, sometimes we do just have to dig in and
work harder. Although I firmly believe we can simplify our
approach, that doesn't mean it won't take hard work and
occasionally long hours and require you to meet more demands.
Power stroking is often necessary.

But what Ernest Singleton and the Decision Pulse studies
teach us is that the power stroke shouldn't be our only weapon
of choice. The combination of power strokes *and* pivots can
amplify our efforts. What we're learning is that the quickest and
most efficient way to drive change—over and over again, as
often as the outside world demands it—is by powering ahead in
some areas while pulling back in other areas. By powering
ahead on academics, while pulling back on sports. By powering
ahead on co-selling, and pulling back on piracy enforcement. By
powering ahead on stabilizing the infrastructure, while temporarily pulling back on the Loyalty Program.

Every time your team needs to shift gears, switch lanes, or
steer clear of troubled waters (pick your favorite metaphor) in
response to a change in your environment, five things should
happen. First, you have to *Anticipate* the change ahead, and
Decide which direction you're going. Then you have to *Align*
your team to make the change with you and give them *Permission* to pursue that direction—and *Test* it regularly to see if
reality still supports your decision. For the acronym-lover

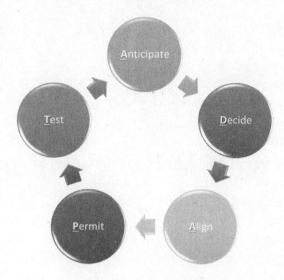

Figure 9.1 The Solution

buried deep inside us all, you can put those five components' initials together to spell ADAPT (Figure 9.1).

And guess what that means? From now on when your friends, family, colleagues, acolytes, sherpas, and caddies ask you what the cool book you're reading is all about, you need only reply, "Glen P. ADAPTs: Great leaders execute new plans by *Anticipating*, *Deciding*, *Aligning*, *Permitting*, and *Testing*." How do you like them apples, Quick Brown Fox That Jumps Over The Lazy Dog?[1]

As you may have noticed already, for your future referencing pleasure, the final chapters of this book are organized into five sections—one for each of the five components in the ADAPT framework. You're welcome.

10

·

Start with ~~Why~~ 13½ Percent

·

WORLD'S MOST BELOVED TOY BREAKS

BILLUND, Denmark, January 7, 2005 – LEGO group, the 72-year-old maker of one of the world's most popular toys, has declared bankruptcy, according to records submitted late yester-day afternoon. The filing comes after a financially troublesome year, and almost a decade of strategic missteps and dwindling brand loyalty.

"We just didn't see it coming," said an unnamed employee as she and her colleagues filed out of LEGO's corporate office shortly after news of the bankruptcy and the corresponding layoffs.

OR AT LEAST THAT'S WHAT THE HEADLINE would have read had 2004 gone differently for the LEGO Group.

That year, the LEGO Group found itself embroiled in a desperate fight for survival. In a surprising move, the iconic maker of one the world's most popular toys, turned to a young strategist named Jorgen Knudstorp. At just 34 years old and nowhere to be found in the family tree of LEGO founder Ole Kirk Christiansen, Knudstorp was an odd choice to be the fourth president in the company's 70-year history.

The first question Knudstrop had to answer was *where do I start?*

With everyone eyeing the future, some argued that LEGO's top priority should be reinvigorating its stale product line. After all, the kids of today just weren't as interested in the old plastic blocks as they were before. And the kids of tomorrow, toting their smartphones and iPads, would almost certainly be even less interested in stodgy old building blocks. Others believed that LEGO needed to get back to focusing on the simple plastic bricks that had made the company so successful in the first place. "Stick to your knitting!" was the rallying cry of this group. One faction inside the company felt its employer needed to do a better job of embracing the digital age with a fresh line of video games and LEGO-themed software. Still another group of concerned Bricksburg citizens offered a convincing case for striking more licensing deals like the wildly successful relationship LEGO America struck with Lucasfilm for Star Wars–themed LEGO's in the 1990s. Then there was the cohort that believed that LEGO's future depended on its ability to custom create its own casts of characters and storylines that would be proprietary to the LEGO Group. On top of all that, it was widely agreed that operational deficiencies and an insular culture of talent recruitment—both resulting from too much success in the company's past—were the primary source of LEGO's ailments.

So which problem was the true root cause?

All of the above.

Buoyed by his training as a McKinsey & Company consultant, Jörgen Knudtstorp jumped head-first into strategy/creation mode. Every night during that bleak January of 2004 when the future of the iconic toymaker hung in the balance, Knudstorp met with Chief Financial Officer Jesper Ovesen for dinner at the LEGOLAND Hotel. Situated right across the street from the corporate headquarters on the edge of the Danish hamlet of Billund, the LEGOLAND hotel was symbolic of the organization's predicament. As a thriving, profitable amusement park on par with its obvious inspiration, Disneyland, the theme park in Billund was one of the brightest stars in the LEGO universe. At the same time, the other LEGOLAND franchises scattered throughout Europe, Asia, and North America were not so lucky. Some were barely afloat. Others were circling the drain. The LEGOLAND brand held so much promise, while it simultaneously caused so much pain. The same could be said for most of LEGO's brands.

CFO Jesper Ovesen was a seasoned executive with a legendary reputation throughout the European business community. In spite of his renown, Ovesen was a numbers guy through and through. He had no designs on the top job at LEGO or anywhere else, so he simply wanted to help Knudstorp succeed. In their work together during the few years leading up to the young president's promotion, Ovesen grew to respect the youthful, personable, and incredibly bright Knudstorp.

But with LEGO being on the verge of crisis, Ovesen pulled no punches when providing feedback. When his peer/protégé sought his counsel on the plans he was concocting, he offered candid critiques. As the CEO-in-waiting, Knudstorp later explained to David Robertson, in his brilliant book *Brick by Brick*, "I had something like eight proposals on what to do about operations, seven proposals for what to do about innovation, and probably seven proposals for market share, and so forth. In all, I must have proposed fifty or sixty actions. And Jesper just looked at me and said, 'The way you describe the company and the way I understand the situation, your plan is too complex. It's never going to happen.'"[1]

Ouch.

Ovesen's advice: focus on survival, not strategy. In practice, these wise words would eventually inspire a notable number: 13½ percent. Every current product, as well as every proposed new product in the LEGO universe would need to describe how and when it would meet or surpass a 13½ percent return on sales.

Suddenly, Knudstorp knew where to begin with the enormous task of saving LEGO. "Jesper's clarity was just what I needed," he said. "But it was also just what the organization needed."

Everyone ranging from the strategist, Knudstorp, to head bean-counter, Ovesen, and every creative director and store manager from Billund to Bloomington knew that the company needed to cut costs, be more innovative, increase sales, and get back in touch with the toy stores that sold LEGOs and the children who played with them.

But what exactly did all that really mean in practice? What direction did that jumble of problem statements really provide for the people on the executive leadership team, let alone the managers elsewhere in the organization? Most importantly, which (if any) of those things would ensure that the LEGO group lived to see 2005?

Suddenly, with the 13½ percent target, managers all throughout the company had a clear guideline for making the tough decisions required of them during that tumultuous year and beyond. Brand managers knew where to allocate resources. Creative teams now had a set of boundaries for their imaginations. Thirteen and a half percent spread through the company like a forest fire swallowing up indecision, and choking the life out of esoteric debates over the supposed importance of this hot initiative or the curve-jumping potential of that new product idea or technological whiz-bang.

A simple number provided the direction they needed. Senior product development leader Paul Shoo explained that the ambitious goal "gave us something to aim for. When I sat down with my product lines and looked out over all of my markets, we always had to ask the question: 'Where do we hit 13½ percent?' It was an incredibly clear way to set priorities."

Hardly a day goes by that newspapers and pundits don't point an accusing finger at some leader or other who was too shortsighted, or one who "lacked vision." You will hear people say that this leader or that plan was too "myopic," which is optometry jargon for people who are literally near-sighted. Indeed many leaders have pushed their companies to the brink of bankruptcy by succumbing to myopia and its cousin, "short-termism."

But the flipside of myopia is hyperopia. And although it is far less publicized, it is just as dangerous. Hyperopia is the scientific name optometrists give to the condition of excessive far-sightedness. Most people need to wear glasses or contact lenses because they have a hard time seeing things far away. People with hyperopia like me, however, have trouble seeing things right in front of our faces.

At the start of 2004, Jorgen Knudstorp was suffering from a temporary bout of hyperopia. Leadership hyperopia comes from having your head and your heart in the right place, but having your eyes in the wrong place.

It can mislead even a high-powered mind like Jorgen Knudstorp's. He was looking too far down the road and seeing every pothole, dip, speed bump, and tight curve for miles to come. When we do that, we overcomplicate the facts. Every risk looks like an immediate threat. Every opportunity is a make-or-break decision. Every challenge takes on the appearance of an intractable problem. From that vantage point, the only logical place to start is *everywhere*. Instead of purifying the small amount of water we need to keep us hydrated, we try to boil the entire ocean.

When you look at the world through a hyperopic lens, every change looks overwhelming. You can't help but conclude that your problems are much bigger than your resources. It feels like you don't have enough of anything—talent, manpower, budget, or time—to succeed.

One great cure for hyperopia is to do what Jorgen Knudstorp did. He checked his thinking with a trusted colleague and clear anti-style, Jesper Ovesen. But sometimes the people around you might be just as overwhelmed as you are, and therefore they offer little help. What do you do then? How do you figure out what your equivalent of 13½ percent is?

The Cure for Hyperopia

WE'RE NOT GOING TO MAKE IT.

That was the disturbing thought facing Tomas Gomez, head of the heavy machinery division of a global manufacturing conglomerate.

Earlier that month, Gomez and his team had laid out their strategic plan, presented it to the corporate planning committee, and received signoff from the steering committee. On paper, it was brilliant. It painted a by-the-numbers picture of how his business unit would grow its earnings by 12 percent from the prior year by executing 18 key initiatives, including the integration of a newly acquired parts manufacturer based in Asia, a sharpening of their positioning for the mining segment, adding new railroad tracks near one of their largest production plants, and becoming the partner of choice for an already huge customer that had just doubled in size thanks to a merger. Oh yeah, not to mention the 13 other soundly reasoned initiatives they could have chosen.

Now if 18 initiatives sounds like a lot, it's because it is a lot. But do bear in mind that this is a global manufacturing business with billions of dollars in annual revenue and 650 managers dispersed among every inhabited continent on earth. The business has a lot of moving parts, to say the least.

The bigger problem, however, is what occurred to Gomez that day. Even if they successfully completed all of these initiatives, they still probably wouldn't reach their earnings target.

The rub is that all those things truly needed to be done. None were merely "nice to have" in the way we commonly use that phrase. When Tomas and his team looked at the future, they saw a sea of sharp-toothed risks ready to attack, and plump opportunities just waiting to be caught if they cast their net quickly enough. Yes, they had singled out 18 initiatives, but they could have added another 20 or 30 objectives to that list without giving it much more thought. Even though they felt that 18 was too many, what could they cut? Every one of them presented a legitimate opportunity for increasing their earnings, or a substantial risk for decreasing their earnings and/or their long-term competitiveness.

For example, they had just spent hundreds of millions of dollars on the Asian parts maker, and this new business alone was supposed to account for nearly 40 percent of their earnings that year. They couldn't just ignore its integration, could they? Then there were the inefficiencies in the supply chain that—if fixed—could yield a few million dollars of new profit every year. Did they really just want to kick that can further down the road? What about the new mega-merging of two of their biggest customers? Certainly that deserved their attention, didn't it?

The same kind of fact-based case could be made for every one of the 18 initiatives on their list. Every single one of those initiatives was important, and led to a tangible dollar amount. That was the problem.

After some sober reflection, Gomez had a revelation. He asked himself a simple question: *If we could get only one thing accomplished this year, what would that thing be?* In other words, what is the one thing that would have a disproportionate impact on everything else this year? After chewing on that puzzling question for a few days, the pieces began falling into place in his mind. At the next meeting of his leadership team, Gomez posed the same question to them.

When they viewed the situation through this lens, one issue stood taller than all others: production capacity.

Their business already had outstanding orders from their biggest customers that they weren't going to be able to fill this year. Why? Because their two largest production facilities were running nowhere near their full capacity. The logic was clear. They were probably going to miss their earnings target by a sizable margin. Yet they had customers waiting in line with outstretched arms and money in their hands. All they had to do was produce enough product in the facilities that were already built to produce at least that much product.

And there it was. Of all the things Gomez's team could do that year, no other objective could match the impact of getting those production facilities to full capacity. It was akin to staying up late at night hatching schemes to make more money to feed your family, when you already have a check in your pocket that just needs to be brought to the bank and cashed.

In hindsight, it sounds obvious, doesn't it? Which is precisely the point. Once he asked the right question it *was* obvious. But had Gomez not asked the question, he and his team would have remained mired in complexity, building out action plan after action plan, and running themselves ragged on the hamster wheel of mindless productivity. The new direction that deserved their focus the most would have either been buried under a pile of possibilities, or drowned in a sea of "important" issues.

●

Let's do an experiment: Make a list of all the initiatives your team is working on right now. When you're done, go to the next page.

●

Got it?

Okay, now, look at that list. Cross off everything on the list that is *not* important.

Now, how many things did you cross off?

If you're like 99 percent of teams, nothing on your list got crossed off. Why? Because every initiative your team is working on right now, or has thought of working on in the future, is "important" to somebody somewhere somehow. You are a smart person. The members of your team are smart people. They wouldn't have suggested doing something that was unimportant. That's why "what's important?" is the wrong question to ask.

A better question is the one that Tomas Gomez asked himself after some sober reflection on the plan: *If we focus on one thing this year, which one will have the biggest impact on our success?*

Think of it this way: If your family was starving and you had a pantry full of canned food, which of the following would be your number one priority?

(A) Find a job.

(B) Find some change in the couch cushions.

(C) Find a can opener.

I don't know about you, but I'm going with "C." Yes, eventually you're going to need to find a source of income. Yes, if you found some coins under your couch, you could maybe go to the store and buy some food: but first things first. You have food right there under your nose. Log off careerbuilder.com, quit ruminating over your resume, stop sorting and resorting your unpaid bills, and *find a can opener*!

●

In some ways, the LEGO group had an advantage over Tomas Gomez's business, because LEGO was on the brink of bankruptcy. As the writer Samuel Johnson said, "Nothing focuses the mind like a hanging." If you're facing tough times and near-death experiences, you can use them to your advantage by letting those circumstances sharpen your focus.

But hopefully, your situation isn't that dire. Either way, you can still achieve that same level of focus by asking yourself Tomas's question: *What is the one thing that will impact our success the most this year?* For Gomez it resurrected a long overdue project they had put off in recent years in order to manage their acquisition-fueled growth spurt.

So did Tomas Gomez's team stop doing everything else? Did they quit integrating the new company they just spent hundreds of millions of dollars acquiring? Did they just say, "To hell with the newly merged mega-customer"? Of course not. But they did put all those other priorities in their proper places on the hierarchy.

After they decided how urgent the capacity project was, Gomez and his team drew in some of their corporate resources to establish a special projects team whose sole goal was getting those plants up to capacity. Within the first few months of the year, they had the plants running the way they needed and were free to reallocate resources back to other priorities on their plan.

That single question Tomas Gomez posed to himself and his team pierced through the layers upon layers of complexity in his multinational business, and exposed the focal point for his team's new plan at that unique moment in time.

Just like the 13½ percent directive at the LEGO Group, answering this question "was an incredibly clear way to set priorities." Gomez's question, however, is not static. It is a question every leader can ask herself over and over again every few months in order to easily anticipate what the next focal point should be. Spotting that next major opportunity or major risk is what anticipation is all about. It is also the first step to creating a more agile and adaptive team.

The Focal Point Discovery Process on the next page can help you answer that question.

Table 11.1 Focal Point Discovery Process

1) Who ultimately decides whether your team succeeded this year? Your CEO? Your Board?	2) What is that decision maker's ultimate objective(s) this year?	
3) List all all the ways your team can contribute to that ultimate objective.	4) Write "E" next to each contribution that can make your team exceptional.	5) Rank the "E" items in order of importance.
6) Write your #1 ranked Value Proposition for this year in the space below		

SECTION 2

•

Decide

•

12

•

The Revolution That Was Televised

•

ONE DAY IN 1997, A PACKAGE ARRIVED at the Santa Monica office of a former comedian and talent agent named Chris Albrecht. Inside the package was a script for a pilot episode of a new TV show which told the story of a relatively successful family man named Tommy who was quietly struggling to make sense of some personal and professional issues.

Albrecht, who was now the senior vice president in charge of the premium cable network HBO's original programming division, and his second in command, Carolyn Strauss, were on the lookout for new shows.

But the Home Box Office team wasn't looking for just any new show. Albrecht's team had devised a plan that hinged on finding a new kind of television show with compelling characters. The kind of compelling character Albrecht and Strauss were thinking of transcended the likes of a crafty, but lovable teenager such as Mike Seaver of *Growing Pains*; the adorably neurotic singles on *Friends*; or even a gruff yet funny blue-collar housewife like *Roseanne* from her eponymous show. A "compelling character," the way the original programming division defined the term, meant a character that was truly *original*— someone unlike anyone you'd find on any television network circa 1997. They believed that a lineup of shows like that would transform their division, and maybe even their company.

During the first few years of Chris Albrecht's tenure at HBO in the late 1980s, the fledgling original programming division— which included everything from boxing matches to made-for-TV movies—held a fairly low spot on the company totem pole. Not only was their offering a departure from HBO's bread-and-butter offering of replayed Hollywood movies, it was also headquartered on the West Coast while HBO's mother ship remained in New York City. That amounted to a double whammy for Albrecht's division.

Nevertheless, despite the California office being regarded by most of HBO's East Coast regime as the home of flakes and weirdos, the balance of power slowly began to shift westward. Fate first smiled on them in 1988 when the Writers Guild of America went on strike. The writers' protest forced almost all of the major broadcast networks to air nothing but reruns. Not so for HBO. Thanks to Albrecht's original programming division, HBO had a fully stocked inventory of fresh new programs to keep their lucky subscribers feasting on new plots and characters while the rest of the destitute viewing population scraped by on outdated episodes of *M*∗*A*∗*S*∗*H* and *The Brady Bunch*.

By the early 1990s, HBO's new programs weren't just available, they were also regarded as pretty darn good even by the most discerning viewers. Comedies like *The Larry Sanders Show, Arliss*, and *Tracy Takes On* were attracting a respectable audience while simultaneously earning a little bit of critical acclaim.

But internally, original programming still had to fight an uphill battle for budget dollars. As one team member at the time, Susie Fitzgerald, explains, "You were always struggling to make the case that this was the way to keep subscribers. In order to eke out money [from the steering committee], we were saying, 'We need continuing characters for the audience to fall in love with, so when they move or something, they don't just disconnect.'"

It was a classic chicken and egg scenario for the original programming team. To prove that a higher volume of compelling characters would increase subscriptions, they needed more money to compete with the major networks for more compelling shows. But mercurial CEO Michael Fuchs was reluctant to give them more money without knowing whether the increased budget would pay off.

Then in 1995, the chief financial officer, Jeff Bewkes, got the nod to replace Michael Fuchs as chief executive officer. Bewkes was much more open to the idea that original series could be vital to HBO's future success, so he began to crack open the coffers, even if only slightly. At the same time, a fortuitous innovation in lightweight satellites spawned a whole new distribution channel for HBO via the services provided by the Dish Network and DIRECTV, in addition to the cable companies. The newly expanded market for HBO enabled Albrecht and his team to pull slices from an even bigger pie of HBO cash.

Still, the original programming team's *more-characters-equal-more-subscribers* argument was difficult to prove to nonbelievers. It was merely a hypothesis. What they needed was an opportunity to prove their point beyond the shadow of a doubt. While some of the shows, like *Larry Sanders*, boasted respectable viewerships, original programming didn't yet have a homerun.

So when Tommy's story was literally hand-delivered to Chris Albrecht, it should have seemed like a blessing. There was a problem with the story, however. That problem clearly explained why the script landed at HBO's office in the first place.

Back then, cable channels simply could not compete with the budgets and significantly broader viewership offered by the major networks. Cable was sort of like junior varsity for the television industry—a demotion for the top talent. So for both financial reasons and reputational reasons, the best writers and their producers didn't want their shows ending up on HBO.

Translation: If CBS wanted a script in 1997, HBO didn't have a chance at it.

The good news for Albrecht and Strauss was that CBS didn't want this script. Neither did FOX, ABC, or NBC. That was also the bad news. None of them wanted the script because the show's hero possessed a tragic flaw. He was a criminal. While that may seem like a silly concern today, a lawless protagonist was unprecedented in 1997. Back then it was regarded as an indisputable fact that a TV hero, even a flawed one, must always be one of the good guys at the end of the day. Otherwise viewers will grow uncomfortable, the audience will disappear, and the show will die.

The original programming team faced a decision. On the one hand, they firmly believed that owning and producing compelling characters for subscribers to fall in love with would be the key to taking them to new heights. But in order to acquire that compelling character, they would have to cut ties with the most basic rules of their industry.

In the end, the team decided to give the show the green light with only one minor adjustment to the original script. Tommy would still be an unapologetic criminal. But Tommy would no longer be "Tommy." He would be "Tony."

When *The Sopranos* debuted in January of 1999, it changed everything. Throughout the show's six seasons, it would win 21 Emmy Awards and five Golden Globes. In 2012, *TV Guide* ranked it as the best television series of all time. In 2013, the Writers Guild of America named it the best written television show of all time. Almost overnight, *The Sopranos* transformed HBO from a second-tier cable TV network into an entertainment powerhouse at which Chris Albrecht and Carolyn Strauss' original programming division became the crown jewel. The dramatic spike in subscriptions to HBO following season one triggered a windfall of profits that surpassed the earnings of all four major networks that passed on the script—CBS, NBC, ABC, and FOX—

combined. As of 2014, HBO and its juicy, industry-dwarfing 36 percent profit margins are the most sought-after property in the media industry. No less than 21st Century Fox, Disney, and Amazon are falling all over themselves to get their hands on what *Bloomberg BusinessWeek* called the "30-year-old cash-printing machine known as Home Box Office."[1]

Original programming suddenly had plenty of respect from HBO's corporate headquarters. And this was that special kind of respect that comes with a blank check for a budget. But perhaps most astonishing is the fact that a channel on *cable TV* — long regarded as the place where good television talent goes to die — instantly became a premiere destination for the most innovative writers and actors in the entertainment industry. The character of Tony Soprano was the black queen of diamonds for Hollywood's top creative talent. It was the current and future team members of the original programming division who immediately recognized Tony Soprano as an unmistakable turn signal.

Albrecht's airing of *The Sopranos*, in spite of the show's direct conflicts with the basic premises of programming success, inspired a bona fide revolution. It was to HBO what the Boston Tea Party was to the American colonists, what a Tunisian street vendor's decision to set himself on fire was to the disillusioned masses behind the Arab Spring, what the storming of the Bastille was to the Jacobins of eighteenth-century France, and what the Salt March was to Gandhi's liberation movement in India.

After *The Sopranos* opened the door, new shows starring complicated anti-heroes like Tony Soprano began flooding television. *Breaking Bad*, *Mad Men*, *The Wire*, *The Shield*, *Dexter*, *House of Cards*, *Orange Is the New Black*, and countless other series continue pouring out today in such a volume on so many different channels that it's hard to imagine a time not so long ago when this type of show simply did not exist.

And it all began with a decision.

●

When we hear the HBO story it's tempting to conclude that Chris Albrecht was just an insanely lucky guy. Time and again the chips just kept falling into place for him due to factors almost completely beyond his control. First, there was the writers' strike in the late eighties that thrust original programming into the spotlight. Then there was the replacement of Michael Fuchs with the much more vision-friendly Jeff Bewkes. There was the innovation in satellite TV that freed up more cash for HBO to place larger bets on more original programming. Lastly of course, we can't forget about the script for the most acclaimed television show of all time being literally hand-delivered to Chris Albrecht's front doorstep.

Obviously, the lesson here is that the big networks were run by myopic idiots and HBO was led by enlightened visionaries, right?

Not exactly.

Even the HBO team had concerns. They were nervous and excited at the same time. As Carolyn Strauss explains in Brett Martin's fascinating book *Difficult Men*, they had serious questions. "Could we have a show with a criminal as a protagonist? I remember sitting in a room with Jeff [Bewkes] and Chris [Albrecht] hashing through it: 'Should we do this? We should do this! *Can* we do this?'"

After a private viewing of the pilot episode of *The Sopranos*, Chris Albrecht's nearly speechless response was simply: "It's really good." Yet even after that glowing conclusion he still waited months, until the very last day before his option on *The Sopranos* expired, before giving showrunner David Chase the go-ahead to create the first season.

But wait a minute. Didn't *The Sopranos* present the very opportunity for transformation that Albrecht had waited almost a decade to receive? Why did he hesitate?

That's the funny thing about revolutionary change decisions. The decisions that inspire our companies and our teams, and that transform our careers and our lives, almost always seem obvious in hindsight. But they almost never feel obvious in the moment.

But fear not. The simple decision framework laid out in the next chapter can dramatically reduce the aspiring change-maker's pain.

13

•

The Pulse, the Anti-You, and the Mindset

•

IN 1955, THE OWNER OF A SMALL toy company in Southern California received a phone call from a television studio executive. The executive told the company's owner, Ruth, about a new children's show his network was launching. He explained why Ruth's company would make a great sponsor for the show, and said all he needed from her was a 52-week commitment at a cost of $500,000. Ruth conceded that it could be a great opportunity, but asked for a chance to think about it before officially saying "yes."

After hanging up the phone, she went to talk it over with her husband and co-owner Elliot. What the television executive didn't know is that $500,000 was equivalent to her and Elliot's entire net worth at the time. On top of that, it was also 1955, just a short few years after the invention of TV started going mainstream. Television advertising was still in its infancy, and it was literally unheard of in the toy industry. No toy company in the world advertised at all outside of the last few months of the calendar year, let alone on television: which is all to say, this was a risky decision. There was no historical data or benchmarking they could tap into. The future was not just uncertain, it was unknowable.

But it also presented a big opportunity. Even back then TV appeared to be changing consumer behavior, and other industries seemed to be getting on board with it. It was like the Internet in 1995—it was changing things, but exactly how it would change things, or what you should do to get in front of that change, was anybody's guess. Some people would get left behind, others would place the wrong bets, and a lucky few would be catapulted to breakout success.

All these risks and possibilities swirled around Ruth and Elliot when they sat down to discuss the sponsorship. The first thing they did was to identify their focal point. They looked out over the landscape of possibilities in an attempt to define the area that would make the biggest impact on their success. A sober look at all the aspects of their business led them to conclude that what made them successful wasn't the efficiency of their inventory and distribution processes, or their customer service, or their relationships with retailers, or even the quality of their products.

The biggest contributor to their success was their marketing ability. That was what I call their "pulse"—the lifeblood of their success. Their competitors' pulse was likely something other than marketing. But for Ruth and Elliot, marketing was the secret to their success at that moment in time. So they had to conclude that if they were going to take a big risk, it should at least be a risk that allowed them to leverage their greatest strength. Since advertising was one tactic that fell under the umbrella of marketing, it was at least a risk that moved them in the right direction.

Next they walked down the hall to the office of their CFO, Yas Yashida. "What is your take on this, Yas?" they asked Yashida.

"Given our current finances," he replied, "if we do this sponsorship and it doesn't significantly increase sales, we won't be broke. But we *will* be very badly bent." So now they understood the risks and implications of each option.

Lastly, they had to decide. Just like Chris Albrecht had to do with *The Sopranos*, they simply had to take a step into the unknown with no guarantees of success and massive uncertainty.

Forty-five minutes after she hung up the phone with the television executive, Ruth called him back and said, "Okay, we'll do it."

As luck would have it, that TV show turned out to be *The Mickey Mouse Club*, and Ruth Handler's little toy company would eventually become the toy giant Mattel. A few years later, Ruth Handler introduced the world to a blonde bombshell named Barbie with plastic limbs and questionable anatomic dimensions. The rest is toy history.[1]

●

If we reverse engineer Ruth Handler's bold move, we'll see that it happened in three parts.

The first thing she did after hanging up the phone was to "check her pulse." She went and found her co-owner/husband, Elliot to determine that marketing was their focal point—the lever they could pull to most significantly impact their near-term success.

Next Ruth and Elliot "consulted their anti-you." They marched down the hall to the office of their CFO—someone who almost always saw things from a different perspective than the risk-taking entrepreneurs did. They weren't deferring the decision to him. They were simply looking for his take on the situation. They were taking advantage of an alternative frame of reference.

Finally, they made the decision. In spite of the uncertainty, Ruth reached a conclusion and made a judgment call with the help of her team. The act of deciding has been dramatically and unnecessarily overcomplicated in recent years. Yes, there were a lot of factors for her to consider when making an investment of this size. Yes, there were any number of ways she could be led astray by irrational quirks of the human mind. All of these considerations are real and valid. But considerations can become crutches. Ruth kicked aside her crutches and made a call.

But don't be confused. This isn't a book about risk taking or about why bold is beautiful. This is a book about dealing with change quickly and effectively. And the three steps Ruth took to make her decision provide us with a highly useful checklist for reaching decisions when you really don't know what's going to happen. But the conclusion doesn't always need to be bold and daring. This would have been a good decision even if she had turned down the offer— because she used a clear process to arrive at her conclusion.

Chris Albrecht at HBO followed the same process when he decided to pursue *The Sopranos*. He thought about his strategic insight that "compelling characters" could not only pave the way to a bright future for his division, but for HBO as an organization. *Compelling characters* became Albrecht's pulse in the way *marketing ability* was Ruth Handler's pulse.

Every step of the way Albrecht consulted Carolyn Strauss, whom he regarded as the perfect partner for him, since they approached things from such different perspectives. While they saw eye to eye on the strategy, they approached each decision from opposing vantage points and personalities.

Finally, Albrecht simply had to make the call about whether or not to greenlight *The Sopranos*. Even though it aligned with the direction of his *compelling characters* strategy, and even though Strauss felt like it was probably the correct turn to make, there was no guarantee that *The Sopranos* would find an audience, let alone become a breakout hit that launched a revolution in television.

If you look closely at all the stories in this book, you'll see this three-step process replaying itself over and over again. Leaders and their teams can use that process to decide which new direction to pursue, as well as for making all those execution decisions before, during, and after a new plan is announced.

If you're a card-carrying member of the Decision Pulse fan club, you are probably already familiar with this three-step process. Regardless of whether you're a neophyte or a veteran, it's worth reviewing again here.

The process starts with checking your pulse. Most often your pulse is going to be the answer to the question: What is the one thing we can focus on this year that will make the most disproportionate impact on our success? For Ruth Handler it was "leverage our marketing abilities." For Chris Albrecht it was "find compelling characters." For Tomas Gomez it was "maximize capacity." For Jonathan Mburu it was "stabilize the IT infrastructure." Whatever your answer to that question, that is ground zero for every decision your team makes this year or until it's time to switch directions again.

In the next chapter, we'll look a little closer at step two.

14

•

Why Drivers Need Navigators

•

WHEN MAKING DECISIONS, OPPOSITES ATTRACT . . . OR AT LEAST they should. Let's face it, we all have blind spots. The only way to beat your blind spot is to find somebody who lives there (your anti-style) and buddy up with them when you need to make a decision. This frenemy is your secret weapon for smarter decisions.

An anti-you can be anybody who thinks differently than you. We need those people close by.

Why?

It's not just because somebody has to be there to annoy us when our families aren't around. We also need them to keep us from driving off the road, from causing accidents, and accidentally ditching the team members who are trying to follow us. Sometimes your anti-you is more or less assigned to you by your functional roles. In hospitals, doctors have nurses and nurses have doctors. Surgeons have anesthesiologists. Entrepreneurs have chief financial officers. Chris Albrecht from HBO had Carolyn Strauss. Glen Peterson from Davis Medical had Priya. Jorgen Knudstorp had Jesper Ovesen. Ruth Handler had her husband and Yas Yashida.

But in some cases, functional roles don't shake out the way you'd expect. About a year into the working relationship with my Chief Operations Officer, Cliff, we discovered just such a disconnect. After hearing me give a presentation on the importance of an anti-you in which I told the Mattel story from the previous chapter, he asked me afterward, "So am *I* supposed to be the risk-averse one in this relationship?"

Oops.

Although Cliff was playing the part of my CFO at the time, he had worked with a lot of entrepreneurs over the years and wasn't terribly risk-averse by nature. I had ignorantly assumed that just because he was considerably more experienced than me, and because I asked him to play the role of part-time CFO, that he would automatically be the cautious pessimist who would rein in my visionary tendencies. (And by "visionary" what I really mean, of course, is "irresponsible, scattered, and spacey.") While functional roles and other superficial characteristics are usually a good starting point for identifying your anti-you, just be wary of overgeneralizing.

A better way is to use your decision style. Remember what your decision style was? Take a look at Figure 14.1 to find out who to look for to be your anti-style. Then get into the habit of consulting with that person, or someone like that person, when you're making decisions.

You can think of this anti-style as your navigator—and, yes, occasionally your backseat driver. Navigators help you drive better in two ways. They help you make smarter turns ahead, and can also look behind to make sure everyone else is still following you.

My Style	Who am I?	My Anti-Style
Farmer	Your decisions are the product of diligent, often unglamourous work. But you know the future is as unpredictable as the weather, so might as well take some risks.	**Investor** *"Daily chores aside, are you sure you're even in the right field?"*
Fisher	You get in your boat and brave the storm every day, fully aware that your decisions may or may not work out due to factors way beyond your control. C'est la vie.	**Thinker** *"Really? C'mon, think this through."*
Builder	You know that Rome wasn't built in a day, but with one carefully placed block at a time. You make decisions with that lesson in mind.	**Hunter** *"Yeah, but I'm hungry right now!"*
Manager	The devil is in the details. But you've got deadlines to meet. So your decisions are a constant battle between speed and caution.	**Inventor** *"Chill out and imagine the possibilities..."*
Inventor	Like your cousin the hunter, you're willing to bet on the long term. In spite of the near-term risks, you are okay with patiently working through decisions.	**Manager** *"Big thinking is good, but how about you just get something done today?"*
Hunter	With decisions, you know that you win some and you lose some. So you choose to place your bets on long-term opportunities, and adapt along the way.	**Builder** *"Easy there, killer. What about tomorrow?"*
Thinker	Livin' on the edge is not your style. Before deciding, you like to look at the big picture and make sure you've considered all options.	**Fisher** *"If you wait for perfect conditions, you might starve."*
Investor	You try to get a bird's-eye view of a situation before deciding. You're also skeptical of "great opportunities," and rarely hesitate if your gut tells you to walk away.	Farmer *"You can't outthink the future, but sometimes you can outwork it. So get busy!"*

Figure 14.1　Anti-Styles

The driver already has plenty to think about just keeping an eye on the road ahead and anticipating what's coming next. The navigator has a different vantage point and often a different set of responsibilities. For example, as the entrepreneur at her company, Ruth Handler's job was to spot opportunities and keep pushing to realize her vision. She was focused on the future. As chief financial officer, Yas Yashida's responsibility was to keep the company financially healthy. This healthy tension is what allowed the company to keep plowing ahead without running out of gas. It also allowed Ruth to feel more confident in her decisions, knowing that Yas was mindful of her inherent blind spots as a reward-seeking entrepreneur.

In other cases, the navigator can help keep a closer eye on the train of cars following you. At Davis Medical, that was the role Priya played for Glen Peterson. Drivers also have a responsibility to check the rearview mirror, but Glen Peterson had to devote most of his attention on the path ahead so that he didn't cause the whole caravan to career off the road. Priya's position in the division gave her a clearer view of where the rest of the team was at that time. She further leveraged that vantage point by consulting with her own direct reports to check their view of the new plan. She was able to call attention to a part of the trip that Glen hadn't noticed—namely that the rest of the team didn't notice him turn on his blinker.

Finally, after you check your pulse and consult your anti-you, there is just one thing left to do: decide.

This last step of actually grabbing hold of the wheel and making the turn is as much an act of faith as it is a logical calculation. Achieving clarity about your pulse and diligently covering your bases by consulting with one or more anti-yous should give you more confidence in the eventual decision. But the real world—the place that exists outside case studies, textbooks, and laboratory experiments—will always be one part unpredictable and one part unknowable. That's why, in the real world, real leaders simply have to make tough calls. Everyone is capable of making those calls, but it sometimes requires summoning the most courageous version of ourselves. So how do we do that?

15

•

To Lead Is to Decide

•

IN 2005, *FORTUNE* MAGAZINE NAMED RUTH HANDLER'S decision to sponsor *The Mickey Mouse Club* one of the five best business decisions of all time. Indeed, it all worked out magnificently for Ruth and for Mattel.

But I want to take us back now to the start of 1955, right after Ruth returned the call to the executive from ABC and told him that Mattel would love to sponsor the show. After the initial excitement faded a few days later, probably after they had to write that first six-figure check to ABC, another emotion crept in.

Fear.

Fear that the sponsorship cost too much money. Fear that this new show would fail. Fear that television wasn't as big a deal as everyone thought it would be. Fear that they were too rash in their bold decision. Fear that sponsorship wouldn't translate into purchases. Fear that they were just plain wrong.

Three months into their new arrangement, to reward Ruth and Elliot for their leap of faith and to allay their fears and doubts, guess what happened?

Nothing. No spike in sales. No additional phones ringing or orders being placed. The silence was deafening.

Six months later, guess what happened? Still nothing.

Nine months later, more of the same. Nothing.

Then finally, after a painstaking year of trying to keep their spirits high and their blood pressure low, while they fought the good fight one decision at a time, the fourth quarter rolled around. And with the fourth quarter came the holiday shopping season. All of the sudden, demand exploded and it didn't let up for decades.

So often in these tales of greatness, history forgets the excruciating nine months between the time Ruth made this decision and the time when she and Elliot saw any reward or feedback for it. During that time she and Elliot still had a business to run and a life to lead—both of which required even more decisions. In addition, she had to go to the office every day and look her employees in the eyes, knowing full well that she might have made a decision that would send every one of them to the unemployment line. She had to look at Yas Yashida every day wondering with every conversation whether there was a hint of *I told you so* in his voice, or a judgmental glint in his eye.

The way history remembers this story is that the Handlers made a great decision in 1955 that caused Mattel to leap to the top of their industry almost overnight. However, when we recount the story like a photomontage with the *Karate Kid* theme song playing in the background, skipping from one big event to the next, where mere seconds separate the start of a nine-month period and the end of it, I think we do ourselves a disservice. We gloss over the most crucial part. We miss the part where the Mattel team had to continue decisively and positively doing their jobs in spite of unyielding uncertainty, not just for a few weeks or months, but for 270 sleepless nights in a row.

All these years later, we can and should look back in admiration. We absolutely should learn something from Ruth's decision. But we need to admire it with our eyes wide open. We shouldn't let ourselves fall into an expectation trap in which we believe that if we could just emulate Ruth's decision or Chris Albrecht's decision then our health, wealth, and happiness would be inevitable; or that the stresses of leadership would melt away and our success would be instant. It rarely works that way and if we expect it to, we are setting ourselves up for failure.

I'm not trying to be Denny Downer here, but leadership decisions almost never work out that way. (Would you believe that I'm sometimes referred to as an "inspirational speaker"? My grand finale is "someday you're all gonna die." Seriously.)

Truth is that, aside from a handful of exceptionally high-profile decisions that account for a mere fraction of a fraction of 1 percent of all the decisions you'll make in your lifetime as a leader, almost all of them will be met with deafening silence for days, weeks, or months after you make the call. The loudest response you'll hear is the echo of your own voice.

In spite of all that, the leader's primary responsibility is to make judgment calls. Depending on how you look at it, that can be empowering and exciting or it can be draining and over-whelming. There is no magic solution. There is only a mindset that must be fed and nurtured on a regular basis. (Read Chapter 5 again for a refresher.)

The Decider's Credo is one tool that some people find helpful, and that I'm sure others find silly. Since the decider's mindset is really just a set of beliefs, I created the credo as a reminder of what those beliefs are—a primer for your brain—that you can refer to whenever you're struggling to decide.

- I am a decider. I start each day with one critical mission: to take decisive, directed action. I define my direction and I act decisively in that direction every day.

- I am a decider. I charge into the unknown hundreds of times every day. I do not shrink from action, even when I have incomplete information. I always exercise good judgment, but I never let fear of the unknown paralyze me.

- I am a decider. I understand that indecision is toxic. I understand that the purpose of a decision is not to hunt down the perfect option, but to get to the next step in a long journey.

- I am a decider. I accept that I will make mistakes. I accept that I will fail. And I accept that if I never make mistakes or fail, I will never truly succeed because I'm just not trying hard enough.

- I am a decider. I can't control or predict the future. Even so, my decisions count. My decisions shape my reality. Decisive action is my greatest asset.

- I am a decider. I am decisive because people depend on me. I am decisive because I want to make my life matter. I am decisive because I want to do something meaningful.

- I am a decider.

Now if this strikes you as pop psychology self-help mumbo jumbo along the lines of Stuart Smalley's daily affirmation (*I'm good enough, I'm smart enough, and doggone it, people like me*) that you are clearly too smart for, then feel free to scoff and ignore at your leisure.

But you have my solemn vow that this will be our little secret if you want to keep it handy for private viewing when you are positive that nobody is looking. (Shhh. . . . Go on. I won't tell.) If you do look at it regularly, you might just find yourself prepared to make some pretty impactful decisions that you never could have seen coming.

One morning in 1995, Rich Lloyd, the district manager of Home Depot stores in Oklahoma City, made a call to the community services director, Suzanne Apple, back at the Home Depot corporate office in Atlanta. With notable urgency in his voice, Lloyd proceeded to tell Apple that, less than one hour before, tragedy had struck. A bomb had leveled the

Federal Building in downtown Oklahoma City, likely killing or seriously injuring everyone inside.

"I just wanted to let you know," he continued, "that we've rounded up all the buckets, shovels, garbage bags, garbage cans, and dust masks in all the stores in our district, and they're all on trucks right now headed over to the bomb site." Lloyd went on to explain that the very least his team could do to make a difference in the face of this horrific tragedy was to make sure that the emergency rescue workers had all the supplies they needed the moment they showed up on the scene.[1]

What's remarkable about Rich Lloyd's bold decision that morning is that the Home Depot, like all big box retailers, was enormously cost conscious. You and I get extra low prices on lumber and light fixtures because they buy in bulk and sell at razor-thin margins. Yet here we have this one middle manager—one whose pay depends largely on his district's financial performance—giving away $70,000 of merchandise in a single morning. Not only was he likely sacrificing part of a bonus check and potentially stunting his career growth, he was risking immediate termination. When he woke up that morning and considered the choices he might have to make that day, you can bet this one was not on his radar.

Yet, in spite of those personal and financial risks, he made the decision. Although he wasn't calling to ask for permission from the home office, he hadn't gone rogue either. In fact he was doing exactly what we all want good leaders to do in tense and tumultuous times. He was acting decisively for the good of his team and his customers—all the while staying in close communication with the people who would be necessary to support his decisions.

In the end, his quick and courageous decision helped restore some semblance of order to a deeply tragic and chaotic situation—which earned him immeasurable good will from the community while showing his employees what the company stood for. As an added bonus—although he couldn't have known it at the time—it also ended up earning Lloyd a promotion.

What makes deciders special is not a naïve belief that they can control all their circumstances or a Panglossian conviction that their decisions can prevent bad things from happening. Instead it is a belief that even when truly bad things happen, they have the ability to step up and deal with even the most horrifying circumstances, one decision at a time.

SECTION 3

•

Align

•

16

•

Rosa Parks and the Science of Revolution

•

ONE MORNING IN THE SPRING OF 1955, an African American woman climbed aboard a city bus in Montgomery, Alabama, during the hustle and bustle of rush hour. Not long after taking her seat, the bus began to fill up. Eventually, the seats in the white section at the front of the bus were all taken so the driver, Robert Cleere, stopped the crowded bus and ordered three young black women to give up their seats to a few recently boarded white women. When one of the African American women refused to move, Cleere flagged down a pair of police officers.

"Who is it?" one officer barked.

"That's nothing new," Cleere said pointing dismissively to the woman. "I've had trouble with that *thing* before."

"Aren't you going to get up?" the two officers asked her.

"No sir," she muttered.

"Get up!" they shouted.

Tears welled up in her eyes as she raised her voice at them. "I paid my fare, it's my constitutional right!"

Each officer grabbed one of her arms and hoisted her into the air, sending the books on her lap flying into the aisle. The event was a first for both of the young officers, still in their mid-twenties, and so they weren't exactly sure what to do. After debating for a few moments, they decided to handcuff the woman and dragged her out of the back of the bus and into the back of their squad car.

On the way to the city jail, they harassed and humiliated her. The two men took turns guessing her bra size and making degrading remarks about her body. Alone in the back seat, she refrained from shouting back. She closed her eyes and tried to drown them out with prayer: *Our father, who art in heaven. . . . I will fear no evil, for the Lord is with me. . . .* The white officers never referred to her by name. They referred to her only as "bitch" and "whore." Eventually she arrived at the jail where other police officers and prison guards continued with the jeers and the taunting.

After what felt like a lifetime, the woman's pastor, Reverend H. H. Johnson, came to bail her out. By that time she had stopped fighting back the tears and found herself weeping like a child. Years later she would recall with pride the words Reverend Johnson spoke to her on the drive back to her King Hill neighborhood. "I'm proud of you," he said. "Everyone prays for freedom. We've all been praying and praying. But you're different—you want your answer the next morning. And I think you just brought the revolution to Montgomery."

Indeed she was the first person to put her fear and personal safety aside and take real action against Montgomery's bus segregation statute. Today, everyone knows that Rosa Parks' decision to stay seated inspired a revolutionary change that eventually ended racial segregation in America.

There is just one problem with this story: Rosa Parks wasn't there.

In fact, Mrs. Parks was at home getting ready for work when the first African American woman openly defied segregation on a Montgomery bus. That young woman was a 15-year-old high school student named Claudette Colvin.[1] A month after Ms. Colvin defied the unjust law, an 18-year-old woman named Aurelia Browder followed suit. Then came Susie McDonald, who was followed by Jeanette Reese, and then Mary Louise Smith. Finally on December 1, a full nine months after Claudette Colvin's brave act, Rosa Parks became the *sixth* African American that year to take a rebellious stand—or *sit*, as it were.

And yet today, it is Rosa Parks who is known as "the mother of freedom."

Why?

The short answer is that Edgar Daniel Nixon, the president of the Montgomery chapter of the NAACP, made a change decision.

•

THE MOBILE MIDDLE AND THE EDGY ELITES

Prior to that fateful spring morning in 1955, Edgar Nixon had spent months anticipating an opportunity to openly challenge the bus segregation law in Alabama and potentially use that as a major stepping-stone to launch a much broader movement. Support seemed to be gathering. But he wanted to transition the civil rights movement to the next level. Nixon intuitively knew that if his group of activists in Montgomery were going to change their city, let alone their state and their nation, they would need to spark action from the throngs of dissatisfied but still largely inactive masses of African Americans, as well as sympathetic—or at the very least *curious*—middle, class white Americans. They needed to send a new signal to these people. Then one day, out of the blue, Claudette Colvin's courageous act seemed to give Montgomery's change leaders exactly what they had been looking for.

Problem was that same spring the 15-year-old Colvin became pregnant.

Social scientists who have spent the past century and a half studying political revolutions have found that successful change movements must tap into at least three key factors—a disillusioned middle class (a mobile middle); a subset of the nobility and intellectuals who are part of the elite class of society, but who don't conform to the values system of their social class (edgy elites); and then some sort of unifying motivation that articulates the cause in such a way that it brings the two dissenting groups together to work toward the same cause (a rebel yell).[2]

All three of these factors were at play in Nixon's decision to make Rosa Parks the face of revolution instead of Claudette Colvin. In the modern era of *16 & Pregnant* and *Teen Mom*, Ms. Colvin's status as an unwed teen mother might not seem like such a big deal. But in 1955, it would almost certainly have created a stumbling block for many of the more morally conservative, yet socially sympathetic revolutionaries among middle-class blacks and whites. Many would-be supporters around the country who didn't fully understand the magnitude of the discrimination in Alabama might have written off Colvin—and the movement she represented—as merely a band of troublemakers and rabble-rousers trying to stir things up and grab headlines.

Rosa Parks, however, sent a very different message. That was no accident.

"The storyline that quickly emerged about Mrs. Parks as a ladylike figure, a woman who had worked all day and was simply too tired to move when she was ordered to get up out of her seat was itself an effective tactic," wrote Fred Gray, the young African American lawyer who represented both Claudette Colvin and Rosa Parks in court. With her horn-rimmed eyeglasses and her neatly groomed hair, her conservative dress, and her soft facial features, Rosa Parks looked like an ordinary, hard-working, middle-class American wife. She looked like your neighbor or your mother or your sister, maybe even your child's Sunday school teacher, the local librarian, or even *you*. Rosa Parks presented the image of a person who would make ordinary folks all over the country sit up and take notice if they saw her on the front page of the morning newspaper getting hauled off to jail in handcuffs.

Nixon's decision *not* to trumpet Claudette Colvin's case also signaled an internal change for the burgeoning movement. It told the other members of Montgomery's local NAACP chapter that a blind passion for justice was no longer enough to make their movement succeed. His decision signaled that they would now align themselves around a carefully orchestrated, highly inclusive strategy directed at the kinds of people that the movement had failed to attract before—the everyday person, rather than only the highly informed and uber–socially conscious activist types.

On top of that, Nixon also recognized the need to involve a reasonable percentage of influential, upper-middle-class members of both the black and white communities—the edgy elites. The mobile middle alone rarely have either the money or the influence to overturn the ruling regime on their own. That's true for organizations, communities, and entire nations.

Think once again about the American Revolution. Without the money, influence, and organizing capacity of the rebellious colonial *elites* like Benjamin Franklin, Thomas Jefferson, and Sam Adams' cousin John, the militias and plucky frontiersmen would have been little more than persistent thorns in the side of King George. They would have been a nuisance and maybe even a bona fide terrorist cell, but not a revolutionary force. They would have been irritating to England only in the way a mosquito is annoying right before you squash it. With the support of some influential elites, however, everything changed.

Even though popular history presents America's founding fathers as ordinary, everyday *aw shucks* kind of guys, they were in fact the aristocrats of their era. Ben Franklin, the creator of *Poor Richard's Almanac*, was anything but poor by the time the seeds of revolution were being sown—by many estimates he was the richest man in America. George Washington was the wealthiest landowner in Virginia. John Adams was a Harvard-educated lawyer. Thomas Jefferson was a lawyer, scientist, philosopher, and plantation owner who fluently spoke six languages. John Hancock was the wealthiest merchant in the country rivaling Ben Franklin for wealthiest person overall. Even though all except Thomas Jefferson came from humble roots, as adults the Founding Fathers were all part of the influential ruling class. What history and social scientists have proven overwhelmingly is that grassroots movements led exclusively by "commoners"—no matter how much we like to romanticize them in our storytelling—never succeed without eventually securing the support of more influential members of society or the organization.

This is the truth that Edgar Nixon intuitively knew when he made his decision about Claudette Colvin. He knew that revolutionary change can and often should start from the average people lower down in the hierarchy—whether those people are Marx's oppressed peasants in industrial societies or the front-line workers in big organizations who have the best line of sight to ever-changing customer needs. But the change movements can't stay in the middle. Eventually, every revolution needs to social climb. It has to crawl up the social hierarchy and reach a subset of thought leaders and power-wielders who have a naturally rebellious streak or some other reason to sympathize with the mobile middle's cause.

Earlier in the civil rights movement the edgy elites included people like the decidedly intellectual and outspoken former first lady Eleanor Roosevelt whom Edgar Nixon had coincidentally bumped into on a train car he was working in after writing letters to her requesting her support for a USO branch for black servicemen in Alabama. It was also people like Clifford Durr, a wealthy white former Rhodes scholar who practiced law in Montgomery and supported his wife Virginia's full-time activism in the community.

In order to reach a critical mass, the movement would require both the mobile middle and the edgy elites working toward the same end. What they still needed was a rebel yell—a unifying motivation that channeled all the angst and discontent and diverse ideologies into a single cause. That was no easy task. Even within the tiniest subsets of the group, disagreements were rampant. For example, at a meeting of local black ministers in Montgomery there was disagreement about how far to push the white power structure. Some wanted full cooperation with the white leaders and feared a harsh backlash, while others wanted to stand apart and not compromise their convictions for anyone—especially white leaders. The impasse threatened to stop the bus boycott in its tracks just days after Rosa Parks was arrested. Only when a charismatic 26-year-old minister named Martin Luther King, Jr. stood up to say he wasn't afraid of the backlash, did the group forge ahead.

To overcome future ideological and practical skirmishes like this, the group needed something that all strata of the loosely connected community could get behind, without their differences getting in the way. That *something* turned out to be a *someone*: Rosa Parks. Like Tony Soprano's character, she was the unexpected black queen of diamonds that caused Americans to reconsider what they thought they knew about race relations in their country.

Even though you might not have your heart set on a coup within your organization, we can still take a lesson from the study of political revolutions. Every change movement inside an organization needs an executive sponsor (an edgy elite) and a group of people—whether a department or a project team or an employee base—to move the change forward (mobile middle). To align both sets of constituencies you need a common focal point that both groups understand and care about.

Effective change leaders in organizations today are able to align people both from the bottom up and from the top down.

17
•

How to Break a Bottleneck
•

NOT LONG AGO, I WAS FACILITATING A decision workshop for the business technology department within a European bank. We were barely an hour into the session when it became abundantly clear that there was an even bigger problem we should be solving. The department head, Carol, explained how this team's biggest challenge was inspiring clear decisions from people two or three levels above them in the organizational hierarchy—people whom they had no authority over.

I had conducted numerous workshops for this company in the preceding years all aimed at helping these teams do their work more strategically and decisively. But a significant restructuring had taken place in the months leading up to this session. The parent company had been centralizing decision authority slowly but surely for years. Little by little, every year, the layers of middle management grew thinner and thinner, and more and more decisions were made at the home office thousands of miles away. At the time of this workshop, it suddenly became clear to us all that virtually no major decisions happened in this regional office anymore.

The good news is that I had been asked to help with this trend in other financial services companies, so I wasn't completely blindsided by it. This trend toward flattening and centralization has been happening all over the world in virtually every industry for the past 20 years or more. So they weren't the first ones to find themselves trying to align people above them far more often than they were aligning people below them. So we took a break and switched gears from "how to be a decider" to "how to be a recommender."

The three rules of getting other people to make a decision based on your recommendation are clarity, clarity, and clarity.

●

CLARIFY WHAT YOU'VE DECIDED IS THE BEST OPTION

Often people do such a good job of researching the situation, looking at it from so many different angles, and thinking so deeply and critically about it that they get lost. By the time they need to make their recommendation, their head is spinning and they have trouble climbing their way back out. As a result, they walk into the executive sponsor's office without really being clear about what they think, let alone what the sponsor should decide.

Before you present your recommendation, pull out a blank sheet of paper and draw a line down the middle. In the left column write down which option you recommend. In the right column write down which alternatives you are rejecting. Why? Because this forces you to make a real decision about what to recommend instead of drifting into a book report about your research. Making a recommendation is not about reporting what you discovered. It's about deciding what to do next.

Rule of thumb number 1: Every recommendation you make must be preceded by a decision you make.

•

CLARIFY THE PRESENTATION OF YOUR RECOMMENDATION

As frustrating as it can be to feel like your progress is at the mercy of someone else, there is also a quiet comfort in knowing that you have a scapegoat when progress stalls. In a misguided attempt to be thorough and/or avoid accountability, we present a slew of options and reams of research instead of standing behind one clear recommendation. The reason why is simple: If we decide to support one recommendation, and the executive sponsor chooses that recommendation and things go south, we might be held partly responsible. But as long as we give seven or eight options, we feel like we can wash our hands of the situation if something goes wrong. After all, we offered plenty of other alternatives—it was the *sponsor* who made the wrong decision. (*See, I really should be in charge!*)

But you can't lead if you can't decide. That's true even when the decisions you make are sometimes wrong. In our misguided attempts to be "thorough," all we've really done is abdicated our responsibility and passed indecision up the chain of command. As a result, the person who is the holder of the bottleneck (who needs to make a decision in order for you to move your project forward) is completely overwhelmed by the number of options you've given them.

It's also helpful to remember that the decision you need this sponsor to make—the one that you've been focused on for weeks—is just one of 40 or 50 decisions that executive sponsor will have to make *that day*. So, by the time you come waltzing into their office with a comprehensive report on the exciting history of accounting software that you've been immersed in for months, this executive might not even remember that your project even exists until halfway through your presentation. At this point the executive sponsor will be so confused and bored, that they won't be paying attention when you reach your exciting conclusion. The more information you vomit onto their desk, the longer you're going to have to wait for a decision.

Rule of thumb number 2: Start with the ending. This is not a Hollywood movie — you don't get extra points for building up suspense before revealing your cage-rattling insight that Acme software 3.2 is a better option for this department than Acme software 3.1. In one or two sentences clearly state your recommendation. Then, after you have briefly described a few of the other possibilities that you do not favor, end your presentation by clearly *restating* your recommendation.

●

CLARIFY THE DEADLINE FOR THE NEEDED DECISION

If you've followed the above two rules, you've made it much more likely that you'll get a timely decision. You will have actually helped them make a decision instead of making the situation more complicated for them.

That being said, I know you can't force a timely decision from someone higher up on the food chain. But there is a subtle, yet highly effective way of getting the executive to commit to a timely decision.

Rule of thumb number 3: Ask them for a specific time and day.

Here's how this conversation would go. At the end of your meeting, you ask: "Are you leaning one way or the other?"

Executive: "Your recommendation sounds good. I'll need to sleep on it and then maybe a few days to look at some things."

You: "Great, is there any other information I can provide to help you with that?"

Executive: "No, this is a very comprehensive report. Uh . . . I should have a decision in the next few days."

You: "Okay, great! Today is Monday, so Thursday about noon then? Would that give you enough time?"

Executive: "Uh . . . let me look at my calendar. Actually, I'm in meetings all day Wednesday and Thursday."

You: "No problem at all. Friday morning then?"

Executive: "Yeah, sure. Friday morning."

You: "That sounds good. I know you're super busy so I'll send you a quick note on Thursday afternoon to remind you."

Now, you have successfully planted a time-based bookmark in your sponsor's brain while also giving yourself permission to follow up with the executive without being a nag.

●

Much of the misguided attempt to be thorough comes from a good place — an inherent desire to do good work. In practice that means we focus too much energy on making a good *recommendation*, and not enough energy on helping that other person make a good *decision*. Remember that a great presentation and even a spot-on recommendation is completely useless if it doesn't yield a good decision from that other person. So try remembering that your objective is not to "make a good recommendation." Your objective is to "inspire a good decision."

My clients find that the distinctions below help get their heads in the right place before delivering a recommendation.

Your goal is to make it as easy as possible for the executive sponsor to make their decision. Your goal should not be to try to knock the sponsor's socks off with a really super fantastic presentation that makes you look super duper smart! You're not in school anymore — so an A+ report doesn't matter: only the result matters. The dirty little secret is that 9 out of 10 times the executive would rather have you make the decision for them. Not because they are lazy, but because they already have plenty to worry about, and, frankly, this project just isn't that

	Good Recommendation	Bad Recommendation
Goal	• To help another person make a good decision.	• To create a killer presentation! • To avoid accountability. • To cover my own rear.
Personal Motive	• Satisfaction of knowing that I enabled a good decision.	• Fear of looking dumb. • Fear of missing something. • Recognition for my hard work.
Presentation	• Concise • Clear • Focused on *their* decision.	• Long & complicated • Wishy-washy • Focused on *my* research.
Result	• A good decision.	• A bad decision.

Figure 17.1   Good Recommendation/Bad Recommendation

high on their own priority list (sorry). So the closer you can come to giving them a decision that they can basically rubber-stamp, the better your chances are of getting a timely decision.

I'm not saying that you don't need to be prepared or that you should cut corners on your thinking and your research. What I am saying is that the executive decision maker doesn't need to know all the details and dead ends on the exciting journey that led to your recommendation. If they have questions, they will ask you. But don't volunteer a dissertation when all they really want is a postcard.

Using the diagram shown in Table 17.1 can help you organize your thoughts into a concise recommendation that resonates with the primary decision maker.

Table 17.1   Good Recommendation Template

Decision Maker Who are you giving the recommendation to?	**Pulse** What is their ultimate strategic objective for this decision?	
Options Write down the available options	**Risk** Write "R" next to the options that present the *least risk*	**Opportunity** Write "O" next to the options that present the *greatest opportunity*
I recommend		

18

•

Mobilize the Middle

•

IF YOU REMEMBER WAY BACK TO THE Check Your Mirrors chapters, the secret to aligning the people on your team is the 90-day sprint and the waitlist. (The what?) I thought you might ask. So let's refresh your memory.

Once upon a time, 14 chapters ago, in a land not too far away, there was an African telecom executive who needed to save his kingdom from an evil army of competitors and government regulators who were terrorizing the land and (gasp) threatening politicians' reelection prospects. To accomplish this, the wise prince made a decision to focus his knights on fortifying their information technology infrastructure, even at the expense of other objectives that had always been regarded as "top priorities." To make sure this shift happened, he identified only three top priorities for 90 days and put all others on a waitlist. Then he

OUR TEAM **PULSE**: Stabilize the IT Infrastructure

90-DAY SPRINT

1. Stabilize the infrastructure by documenting key customer
    touchpoints

2. Fine-tune customer data protection protocols

3. Implement experiential marketing campaign in coastal region

90-DAY WAITLIST

4. Increase size of enterprise solution branding team

5. Finish market research on urban customer usage patterns

6. Expand business service facilities

7. Digitize new product training materials

Figure 18.1   Mburu Sprint Waitlist

swore an oath to his subjects that he would not send them to the
dungeon if they focused on the top priority even at the expense
of other priorities. Each of his loyal dukes and duchesses swore
the same oath.

Ringing a bell? Figure 18.1 is an example of the document
they filled out.

The simplest way for you to ensure alignment is to have every
person on your team complete a document that looks like that.
Your team's sprints and waitlists should consist of four key
parts:

1. A decision pulse—the single overarching focal point for
   the team this year.

2. Top three objectives for the team over the next 90 days.

3. 90-day sprint for each team member (Figure 18.2).

4. 90-day waitlist for each team member (figure 18.3).

TEAM DECISIONPULSE 2015: _____

90-DAY SPRINT

1.
2.
3.

90-DAY WAITLIST

4.
5.
6.
7.
8.
9.
10.

Figure 18.2   Sprint

Because the sprint and the waitlist will not only align your team, but also make you smarter, happier, and prettier (maybe), let's take a deeper look into why it works.

The short answer has to do with the time-space continuum. Don't worry: we're not going to take a detour into quantum physics. What I mean is that priorities only have meaning within the context of a certain timeframe and within a certain space. Deciding to trim a list of priorities can feel like a Herculean task when you think about a whole team or

TEAM DECISIONPULSE 2015: _____

90-DAY TEAM PRIORITIES

1.
2.
3.

90-DAY SPRINT

Team Member	Team Member	Team Member	Team Member	Team Member	Team Member
1.					
2.					
3.					

90-DAY WAITLIST

Team Member	Team Member	Team Member	Team Member	Team Member	Team Member
1.					
2.					
3.					

Figure 18.3   Waitlist

department (space) over the span of a whole year (time). You might look at the upcoming year and say, *Yeah, but we really do have 87 priorities for the whole organization over the next 12 months!*

The 90-day sprint simplifies the task of prioritizing by shrinking the timeframe from an entire year or all of eternity down to just the next 90 days.

Is there anything magical about 90 days and three priorities? No, not exactly. Your team will not spontaneously combust if you decide on four priorities over a 30-day period. So you should treat 90 days and three priorities as general guidelines rather than irrefutable laws.

However, those guidelines aren't totally arbitrary either. They tap into a kind of sweet spot for human behavior. So before you veer too far off the path, you need to understand a little bit about the psychology underlying the rule.

●

THE NOT-SO-MAGIC 90-DAY WINDOW

The 90-day timeframe is helpful for the same reason why we break big goals down into manageable chunks—it makes them feel less overwhelming and more actionable. Ninety days also fits well within the quarterly cadence of most businesses.

But 90 days is also about more than that. Ever since the 1960s, common wisdom held that it takes approximately 21 days to form a new habit.[1] That bit of folk wisdom was based on an overgeneralization of anecdotal observations from a 1960s plastic surgeon–turned psychologist named Maxwell Maltz. In his book *Psycho-cybernetics* he mentions that "it takes about 21 days for the average patient to get used to their new face." In reality, as modern research has confirmed, it usually takes three times that long—more like an average of 66 days to form a new habit. (Although for some people it can take as little as 18 days and for others it can take as long as 240 days depending on the habit you're trying to develop and the traits of the person trying to develop it.)

In other words, if you really want a certain change to stick in the minds as well as on the hands and feet (i.e., behaviors) of your team, it probably won't happen in a week or even a month—no matter how much you or they would like it to. This was part of the issue that Sandy, the high-tech leader, ran into when she tried to transition her team to co-selling. That wasn't just a new priority, it was a whole new set of behaviors.

The prudent change leader (like you, of course) will spot another takeaway here: Set your own expectations accordingly. Yes, your team can and should start shifting its focus immediately if you've effectively signaled your turn. But it is going to take a lot of hours of conscious effort in the beginning before the new behaviors become automatic. And they will almost certainly backslide during that time. You should fully expect and prepare yourself for a "two steps forward, one step back" process over the first few months.

When your people don't appear to be changing two weeks after they all agreed to fully support the new change and swore that they would, it doesn't necessarily mean that they lied to you.

It doesn't mean that they are withdrawing their support for the change.

It doesn't mean that they are dense, insubordinate, dumb, or lazy (most of them, anyway).

No matter how much they desperately *want* to change, habits don't happen overnight. It's still going to take at least a month or two before their behaviors fall in line with their desires. So you need to be patient. You also might need to do a little micromanaging during that time.

Yes, that's right, I said it. Micromanage the new direction. I love autonomy as much as the next guy or gal. In fact I'm almost pathological about autonomy. But when you're switching directions, autonomy needs to take a backseat to clarity. When kick-starting a change the situation itself will bring with it way too much ambiguity to be a hands-off manager. Clear and decisive transformational leadership can sometimes look like micro-managing, because the shift in focus must happen on a micro-level and not just on an intellectual macro-level. It needs to happen with small actions, not just with sweeping visions. Eventually, the leader can and should back off and give her team some room to breathe. But in the first few weeks, micro-managing progress on the top one or two priorities is not just acceptable, it is essential.

So what about those three priorities?

●

LUCKY NUMBER 3

Three priorities during that 90-day period is not a random number either.[2] A famous series of studies from the early twentieth century concluded that human beings could store about seven pieces of information in our working memory (seven plus or minus two to be specific). That's why telephone numbers were seven digits long, so that they would be easy for Ma Bell's customers to remember by heart. So now you can impress friends and neighbors with useless fun facts about the history of phone numbers. You're welcome.

But what, pray tell, do phone numbers have to do with executing changes in direction?

Everything.

Modern research shows that our working memory isn't quite as robust as we thought. The average human brain can actually store only about three pieces of information in our working memory. This matters because your working memory does most of the heavy lifting every time you or anyone else tries to do something new or different, such as pursue a new set of priorities. Everything that takes conscious effort requires the use of your working memory. In order to make sense of the new sentence that you're reading right now, your working memory has to hold the last sentence in mind so that the story doesn't start over after every period. That's why run-on sentences are so confusing—by the time you reach the end, your working memory forgot what happened at the beginning.

Likewise, every time you scan your email inbox to determine which emails to answer right now with the few spare minutes you have, your brain has to make sense of the possible options by stacking them up against some bigger picture objective. You have to call to mind *what am I trying to accomplish?* Although it feels so good, a clean inbox probably should not be your number one priority. Some of those messages are in fact more important to executing your change than others, and as such they deserve more immediate attention. Your sprint and your waitlist will usually tell you which messages to attack first.

Think of Sandy's team. The focal point or decision pulse for her team was the shift to selling comprehensive solutions instead of enforcing licensing deals. That was reflected on everyone's sprints and waitlists. So when one of her salespeople sees a message relating to a customer account whose licensing agreement has expired, and this other message is regarding a customer who might be interested in a comprehensive solution, they should know what to do. One relates to the sprint priorities, and should be answered now. One relates to the waitlist, and so it needs to wait.

As he continues scanning his inbox, this sales manager's working memory will keep "stabilize the IT infrastructure" top of mind so he can compare each email to that critical big picture objective. On top of that, he obviously still needs to hit his sales quotas. If he adds one or two more priorities, the task of sorting will get more complicated but it will still be within the bounds of his capacity.

In spite of his cognitive horsepower, however, his working memory has a limit. Add a few more priorities to the list of three or four, and his working memory stops working. It simply can't recall and compare seven or eight priorities while he scans his inbox.

So what happens next?

Since his brain is literally incapable of making that many comparisons simultaneously, he has to revert to a different sorting system. Now, his brain shifts into what I like to think of as "call center" mode. In call center mode each email will be answered in the order it was received. In other words, there will be no prioritizing whatsoever. He will diligently knock them out one at a time based purely on chronology with no regard for effort or importance. Same thing happens with every meeting request and every phone call. In the moment, responding automatically to every new message chime and cell phone ring seems like no big deal. In fact, it might even be "productive." After all, each of those emails needs to get answered *sometime*, don't they? And as the great Benjamin Franklin advised us, we shouldn't put off until tomorrow anything that could be done today. That is what productive people do, isn't it?

Yes, that is what productive people do. But that is not what strategic people do.

That difference is more than just semantics. Productivity is about getting things done. Strategy is about getting the *right* things done, and leaving other things *undone*.

When you multiply these daily microdecisions by 100 every single day to account for all the emails, meetings, and phone calls facing the average manager, you find that each day has hundreds of missed opportunities to impact your most important objective during that 90-day period. Now multiply 100 by 20 working days each month and you end up with 2,000 missed opportunities per month. Then multiply 2,000 missed opportunities by the 10 people on your team and you now have 20,000 missed opportunities to move the needle on your primary objectives. Every. Single. Month. Sixty thousand missed opportunities later, at the end of your quarter, you and your team find yourselves red faced and frustrated by the lack of progress on your shift in focus.

The change isn't happening.

This is to say nothing of the burnout costs that accumulate from having every person on your team ending every working afternoon feeling like an exhausted firefighter tumbling out of yet another burning house trying to scrub the sweaty soot off their cheeks. All the while, they know that the whole process will start all over again the very next day like *Groundhog Day*, except that Bill Murray isn't there to make you laugh.

Fortunately, the solution is incredibly simple. A 90-day sprint with no more than three priorities lets you unleash the full strength of your obsessive overachieving tendencies on only the most important strategic objectives, and not on every seemingly urgent issue that drops onto your desk every hour.

19
•
Don't Forget the Waitlist!
•

IF YOU HAVE GOTTEN THIS FAR IN the book and you still don't understand why the *waitlist* is probably the most important part of this whole process, then I have failed you. I am afraid we might have to break up, because there's just no future between us. It's not you, it's me.

Through the waitlist—and only through the waitlist—is where this whole process goes from change by addition to change by decision. I opted to make this little section its own chapter so that every time you come back to the table of contents to reference another part of the book, you might catch a glimpse of this chapter heading and be reminded "don't forget the [insert favorite expletive] waitlist!"

The strategic planning team of a regional insurance company explained to me that the waitlist is essential for combatting what they called the "Minnesota nice filter." What they meant is that far too often the leadership team will go into a meeting and identify the key priorities. Then everyone nods their heads eagerly, basks for a moment in the harmony that only consensus can create, and then goes back to working on all the stuff they were working on before. Never mind that those other things weren't listed as a priority.

Based on my experience, this isn't just a Minnesota problem, or a Midwest problem, it is a West Coast problem, an East Coast problem, a fried chicken and sweet tea Deep South problem, a European Union problem, an African problem, a Brazilian problem, an Asian problem, and an Australian problem. If you don't call out other priorities and projects openly and explicitly that will populate your waitlist, this will happen every time.

So three months from now when you're knee-deep into your new change, and it's just not taking effect, and you are frustrated, staying up nights, calling special meetings, and assembling task forces, trying to figure out what went wrong, scratching your head, and saying to yourself, "Everyone created their sprints, why isn't this working?" please do me and you both a favor. Crack open this book or scroll through your e-reader to find one of the seven copies of *Domino* you purchased and come directly to this chapter. It shall set you free.

Oh, yeah, I almost forgot. One more thing . . .

Don't forget the waitlist!

SECTION 4

•

Permit

•

20

•

The Hardest
Permission to Give

•

NOT LONG AFTER THE LEADERSHIP TEAM AT a manufacturing company I worked with decided that factory productivity was the
single most important thing they could focus on that year, the
company leader ran into a tricky execution decision. In this
case Ted, the member of the leadership team directly responsible for boosting the capacity of the two largest production
plants, seemed to underappreciate the urgency of that project.

Ted continued going about his work in the same way he had
before they identified this as the organization's number one
priority. He wasn't slacking off, but he wasn't exactly making
the necessary headway on the new critical initiatives either. Not
only was he failing to make any notable increases in the two

plants' productivity, he didn't seem to be concerned about it. He didn't reallocate any new resources to it. He didn't ask other members of the leadership team to borrow any of their resources. He didn't even fly to the plant location in Belgium to be onsite for this critical project.

In other words, even though the CEO and his team had decided that optimizing plant productivity was their decision pulse for the year, and that all other projects would be subservient to that priority until it was adequately addressed, Ted couldn't seem to make the turn.

He saw the CEO's blinker. He turned on his own blinker. But he just couldn't bring himself to actually grab the wheel and move from the old lane into the new lane. He kept on driving the old projects and initiatives with the same amount of attention and intensity he had in the months leading up to his team's decision to switch lanes. Most disturbing of all to the CEO was that Ted had been something of a shining star in the organization. He had proven himself to be an extraordinarily reliable general manager in his previous roles.

Yet something just wasn't clicking.

●

Unfortunately, this happens. As a general rule, people as a species just aren't good at leaving things behind even when we've decided it's best to do so. We all come from a long line of hoarders. Our most ancient ancestors couldn't be sure when or from where their next meal would come, so those who saved their leftovers lived longer and spread their genetic seeds further than those who carelessly discarded valuable food and warm clothing without much thought. As a result, thousands of years later we have the powerful psychological phenomenon known as the endowment effect.[1] Most of us are hyperconscious of discarding things that belong to us—things that were endowed to us. That includes our projects and our goals. We may not even like the projects we were working on, but the endowment effect, combined with a good old-fashioned work ethic, inhibits our ability to put those other projects aside if they are only half-completed. It literally hurts—as in: the pain sensors in our brain light up—when we try to leave some objects or pursuits behind. (Incidentally, this potent emotional reaction is why change decisions, as opposed to change additions, snap people out of their unconscious processing modes).

After two months of failed coaching conversations that began as friendly nudges from a nurturing leader and that slowly morphed into clear demands from a stern boss, the CEO still couldn't get Ted back on track. He finally had to make the painful decision to let Ted go.

One of the CEO's hypotheses was that Ted simply wasn't cut out for change leadership. He was an excellent steady-state manager who thrived when asked to keep things running smoothly and to squeeze inefficiencies out of a process, but he wasn't able to drive changes beyond tiny increments. My hypothesis was that Ted's greatest strength—his ability to get things done—was now proving to be his Achilles heel. He had such a powerful drive to get things done that he was constitutionally incapable of leaving anything undone, even when priorities changed and those other projects no longer needed to be done.

We'll probably never know exactly which issue led to Ted's ultimate demise. But my guess is that it was a permission problem.

Permission bridges the gap between alignment and action. It comes in three flavors.

We give our teams permission to focus by defining a sprint and a waitlist, and then swearing a no-retribution oath. If you don't like the theatrics of doing it the way Jonathan Mburu did, that's okay. Make it your own, but just make sure it's clear to your team that they have permission to focus on some things at the expense of others.

In the Align chapters, we covered how to permit our bosses and executive sponsors to make a decision by giving them a clear and decisive recommendation, instead of torturing them with a meandering monologue that drags them through a maze of options.

The last kind of permission is arguably the most difficult kind to grant. You have to permit *yourself* to stay focused on the top priorities even when your impulses are tugging at you to go put out this fire, follow through on that old project, or chase that exciting new idea.

My hunch is that Ted's ultimate demise can be traced back to a self-permission problem. He couldn't bring himself to let go of the old priorities and urgent issues that were holding him back and hindering his focus.

So what then is the solution to the self-permission problem?

21
•

Priori-Time:
The Antidote to Urgency

•

ONE FRIDAY MORNING NOT TOO LONG AGO I did a workshop with the management team of a rural hospital system in the western part of the United States. The purpose of our day together was for me to help get a few hundred of their managers ready to deploy that year's strategy. The day was designed to give these leaders an opportunity to step away from the hectic daily challenges inherent in their jobs throughout the hospital, and to think strategically about the direction of the organization as a whole and of their functional teams more specifically.

When the CEO took the stage her brief presentation was telling. After she welcomed everyone, she began by sharing an update on the highest level strategic issue in the organization at that time—the status of a potential merger with one of the larger healthcare systems in the region. She then immediately followed that update by double-checking whether the emergency room at the main hospital was fully staffed that day.

"What a great metaphor," I thought. Here we are, all the key leaders in the organization assembled together for one day for the explicit purpose of thinking big picture and getting out of the weeds, if only for a small chunk of time. Yet, they legitimately could not ignore the fact that the emergency room still needed to be staffed regardless of how much they wanted, and in fact needed, to be strategic that day. The CEO herself then apologized profusely for having to leave immediately after her introduction because she was required by penalty of law to be deposed in a circuit court in the state capital the rest of that day.

On top of this, at least six or seven times throughout my presentation, I was forced to talk over a hospital-wide announcement on the loud speakers in the ballroom informing everyone of one urgent issue or another. So, naturally, I did what any self-respecting prima donna presenter would do: I ripped the microphone off my lapel, threw it on the ground, and stormed offstage screaming, "I can't work under these conditions!"

Just kidding.

My gracious client contacts nevertheless graciously apologized for all the interruptions anyway. I told them I wasn't bothered at all. In fact, I actually felt grateful for the interruptions. Those interruptions gave me an up close and personal glimpse of what it was actually like for all 200 or so managers in that room to actually apply the skills and frameworks I was showing them—which of course all sounded simple and swell to me—that day in the midst of all the real-world interruptions they are forced to manage every single day. For a brief moment, I was able to walk a few steps in their shoes trying to balance the desire to think strategically with the demand to manage operational details.

Fortunately, I wasn't taken completely by surprise. A few weeks before the workshop, we sent out a survey to all the managers asking them the questions that gave us a better sense of the biggest obstacles to focusing on their priorities and deploying their strategy. By an overwhelming margin, the group felt that the single biggest obstacle to making progress on this new plan would be the never-ending demand to perform triage on urgent issues that crop up every single day. The emergency room staffing issue and the loudspeaker interruptions merely illustrated their multiple choice responses in vivid, living color.

As a result, we spent extra time talking about how to *priori-time* their days. All that priori-time really means is that you devote the first 15 minutes of every workday to the number one item on your 90-day sprint list. Fifteen minutes. That's it. Even if all you do is stare blankly at that number one item for 15 minutes, it will prime that day with thoughts of your number one priority. You simply accept the fact that once the day begins, all hell breaks loose and it is highly unlikely that you will get a chance to hide away and devote any focused, creative time to your number one priority.

But if all 200 managers could devote even 15 minutes at the beginning of each day to the organization's top objectives, they would likely turn up a series of small but highly significant insights that could get the organization moving again. I've found that even on the days when the 15 minutes of priori-time yields no insights, it dramatically increases the chances that an insight will come later in the day. That's because even though our conscious brain bounces around for the rest of the day from one urgent issue to the next, our unconscious brain keeps chugging along.[1]

I experience this strange phenomenon so often when I'm writing a new book, that it's become as important to my writing process as typing and editing. For example, as an attempt at work-life balance (and to keep from sharing Jack Nicholson's fate in *The Shining*) even when I'm holed away writing a new book, I don't allow myself to work on Sundays. I don't open my laptop. I don't check email on my phone. Pretty good, right? Yet, almost without fail, if I'm struggling to figure out where a certain story fits in with the larger narrative of the book I'm working on, or if I'm struggling to make some point within a semi-coherent chapter, guess when the solutions usually come to me? You guessed it—on Sunday. Other times, the solution will just come to me on a day when I'm working with a client team, which prevents me from writing more than a few minutes first thing in the morning that day. That early morning writing primes my thoughts, and even when I shut down my computer, the computer of my unconscious keeps humming with its background processing.

Why does this happen? How do we get answers to questions we aren't even thinking about?

In short, we *are* still thinking about those questions: Just not consciously. At any given moment, our brain does all kinds of processing that we aren't fully conscious of. Even when we sleep, our brain goes to work on thorny issues that our conscious brain just can't seem to tease out in our waking hours. But the reason our brain can pull off this magic trick with background processing is because the focal issue *did* consume our thoughts earlier in the day or the day before. By scheduling focused thinking time about your number one priority first thing in the morning—even if you do nothing but stare blankly at that written priority—you are priming your subconscious pump. Instead of your subconscious brain working on whatever random anxiety or daily urgency happens to pop into your stream of consciousness once the day gets rolling, you are setting your mind to work on the issue you most need to resolve that quarter, that month, or that week. Priori-time is how you manufacture eureka moments. You don't know when the insight is going to come, and when it does finally arrive it will feel totally random. But it isn't random. You helped give birth to it by priming your brain every morning to think about the key issue.

In the pre-surveys we do with client teams, the number one most cited obstacle to executing priorities is not actually a lack of clarity or commitment. It is a perceived inability to concentrate on the top priorities when it seems like so many other things need to be done. Most of the time, what gets in the way of executing a new plan has nothing to do with the new plan. The majority of people understand the new plan. They buy into it, and they believe they are perfectly capable of executing it. What they fear most is the dizzying number of urgent demands that will inevitably arise during the course of their average workday.

Urgency is an artifact of modern work life for every working person. Things come up each day that will distract you. But when you priori-time your day, it's like vaccinating yourself against the urgency virus.

SECTION 5

•

Test

•

22
•
Shift Happens
•

Everybody's got a plan until they get punched in the mouth.
                                                    —*Mike Tyson*

ONE THING YOU CAN COUNT ON AS reliably as death and taxes is that
roughly three and a half minutes after you successfully get your
entire team aligned in a new direction, some change in your
environment will force you to reshuffle your priorities again.
This is precisely what happened to Noney, one of Jonathan's
direct reports. Barely one month after the Nairobi meeting
where he set his priorities and publicly gave his team permission to focus on stabilizing the IT infrastructure, Operation
Storm happened. The details of Operation Storm are unimportant (and a tad confidential), but suffice to say that it com-
manded the attention of Noney's team immediately. They had
known it was on the horizon for months, but it was up to the
government officials to put the ball in motion, and they weren't
giving any advanced warnings.

Sudden new priorities like Operation Storm can create a sticky situation for agile leaders. If handled incorrectly, it can completely undermine credibility. In Noney's case, for example, the last time her team saw her live and in person, she had explicitly placed Operation Storm on her team's 90-day waitlist and then publicly given her team permission to ignore it for 90 days. At the same Nairobi meeting, the other direct reports on Jonathan's team—Noney's peers—had also watched Jonathan say—nay, swear—that nothing was more important for every person in that department than stabilizing the infrastructure.

Not even four full weeks out of the gates, a sudden jerk of the steering wheel like this could have made it appear that Jonathan was going back on his word and that Noney was being either insubordinate, obtuse, or both.

Fortunately, it didn't happen that way.

With the sprint and the waitlist in place, the table was set for just such a shift in focus. On the leadership team's monthly status call, Jonathan and his five direct reports took a few minutes to go through each direct report's sprint and waitlist. When it came to Noney's turn, she and Jonathan were able to explain why Operation Storm had moved from the number six spot to the number one spot on her team's list. It took all of four minutes to explain the change, answer the questions from the rest of the team, make tweaks where necessary to any inter-dependencies on the other leadership team members' priorities, and then move on.

For Noney's part, the reshuffling was also easy. She didn't need to go back to the drawing board and write up an entirely new strategy deployment plan for her team. By moving the number six priority to the number one slot, it just meant that the previous number one became number two, the previous number two became number three, and so on all the way down the list. Everyone on her team instantly understood the change without having to exert weeks of time and energy getting "buy-in" for a new strategic plan.

●

It's a funny thing I've noticed in many organizations. What feels like agility to the people at the top of the organization usually looks like waffling to everyone else. That disconnect comes from the fact that when a leader announces a decision, they are fully aware of the circumstances that might force them to make a different decision at any time. However, they are so consumed with the task of "getting buy-in" that they forget to mention to the rest of the team that all of this is subject to change. They unthinkingly assume that everyone else *obviously* knows about the very real possibility of another near-term shift.

But that assumption is false. Everyone else is *not* aware that another change could be right around the corner. As a result of this subtle miscommunication, when that next change happens, many employees disengage, and ultimately end up mistrusting the leadership abilities of the leader.

The leaders could eliminate so much of this grumbling and frustration simply by announcing the change and saying, "If things change in 30 days, 30 weeks, or 30 months from now, we might need to change direction once again. But until then, we're going *this* way."

23
•
Scientific Management 2.0: From Taylorism to Taslerism

•

IF YOU WANT TO SEE SOME OF the most pleasant people in the world turn rabid, walk into a room of passionate human resources professionals and say, "Frederick Winslow Taylor is my hero."

Frederick Taylor and his methods, known as Taylorism, are commonly regarded as one of the great dehumanizing forces of the Industrial Age. His villainous emphasis on ruthless efficiency made stopwatches a manager's best friend and reduced human beings to little more than the interchangeable parts they assembled as quickly as possible day after monotonous day.

Taylorism is also known as scientific management. That's unfortunate, because the true scientific method could be one of the most rehumanizing forces in the modern working world. It acknowledges the potential of human endeavor while fully accounting for the limitations of human knowledge about the future. What's more, the scientific method provides a brilliantly simple framework for dealing with uncertainty.

At its heart, the scientific method is all about testing hypotheses. It goes like this:

1. We examine the current state of knowledge on a subject.

2. We generate a hypothesis that might explain things that we don't yet know (i.e., an educated guess — and can we pretty please stop kidding ourselves and acknowledge the fact that even data-driven guesses are still just guesses?).

3. We test our hypothesis with experiments whenever possible, or with observations and field studies when controlled experiments aren't possible.

4. We analyze those results and generate more hypotheses to be tested again and again and again.

5. When you've tested enough hypotheses and made enough careful observations, you can craft a theory.

That is science. I believe it should also be management. Only the words need to change. In the realm of management, hypotheses become decisions, hypotheses are tested during execution, and the resulting theories are strategies. Let's call this Scientific Management 2.0. Or just to stroke my ego, feel free to call it Taslerism. But, my fragile ego aside, you should know that I'm actually near the tail end of a long line of managers and thinkers who have been preaching and promoting highly effective and comprehensive versions of Scientific Management 2.0.[1]

The science I'm talking about here is about more than just data collection. Not everything can be reduced to a controlled experiment à la A/B testing on a web page — believe me I wish it could. The science I'm talking about is more a way of thinking. It's about a mindset that is both decisive and change-ready. I'm not advocating a close-your-eyes-and-throw-darts-at-the-wall mindset. What I'm talking about is a system of thinking and leading that is based on, first, making clear decisions to go in one direction and not others, rather than limping along with wishy-washy, hedge-our-bets, straddle-two-lanes-at-once approaches.

Second, we would make sure that we constantly remind ourselves—and one another—that every decision is merely a hypothesis. That means we would spend less time up front reading tea leaves in a vain attempt to make the right decision, and more time actively experimenting in order to make whatever we decide turn out right. No matter how firm and certain the decision seemed at the time, every decision must be regarded as a hypothesis. That means it must be tested by time and circumstances. Sometimes the guess turns out to be wrong, in which case we make another decision and test that one. Other times the guess will be absolutely right based on the state of the world *a month ago*, but now it needs to be adjusted based on the state of things *today*.

If every person in the organization knew that this was the way the organization functioned—if every manager were trained to think this way, then leaders could feel free to adapt to changes with speed and agility, without everyone else on the team rolling their eyes and thinking, "Oh great. A new flavor of the month is upon us. . . ."

With the ADAPT framework I've tried to provide a way for you to apply this mindset to the everyday challenges of leading a team in the midst of constant change. It's possible that this way of thinking and leading could make organizations more efficient while making leaders more agile and work more rewarding.

A boy can dream, can't he?

EPILOGUE: WHEN CHANGE BLOWS

●

ONE FALL MORNING A FEW YEARS AGO near Misty Fjords National Monument in southern Alaska, a 51-year-old electrician from Michigan named Adrian Knopps laid down on a wet, grassy strip of land next to a fallen tree. With the exception of one 2-hour respite, this was the first time in seven days and nights that Knopps had been off his feet. It was also the furthest away he'd been from that tree in five days.

As Adrian Knopps lay down starving and exhausted—with thoughts of his wife and his two children fading in and out of his mind—he knew he might never again get up.

●

A week earlier, Adrian Knopps and his friend Garret Hagan, a 24-year-old native Alaskan, set out on a week-long hunting trip in an enclosed, seafaring fishing boat. A day later, they arrived at the mouth of a river in the Misty Fjords National Monument. That Sunday afternoon, the pristine forest greeted them with bright sun and 60-degree temperatures. It was a postcard moment with clear blue skies hanging above snow-capped mountains and lush forests stitched together by glacier-fed streams, all running down to meet the crisp saltwaters of the North Pacific.

After anchoring the boat in the harbor, Hagan and Knopps climbed into a small flat-bottomed skiff designed for river travel. It wasn't long before Hagan sacked their first bear just a mile down river. Both avid hunters, Hagan and Knopps skinned the huge animal, bagged the meat, and loaded it onto their seven-foot skiff before trolling back toward their main boat, still bobbing on its anchor in the harbor.

The 600 pounds of pelt and meat, however, was so heavy that the top of their skiff was just an inch above the river's surface. While the skiff could afford to dip that low in the calm river waters, it would be far too unstable for the rough ocean waves they would shortly encounter in the harbor surrounding Hagan's ocean-fishing boat.

In order to lighten the load on the small skiff, they decided that Knopps would wait on the riverbank while Hagan made the short trip out to his boat to drop off the bear. Knopps took in the beautiful scenery surrounding him while glancing every so often at Hagan slowly receding into the distance until he was little more than a small speck next to the main boat. Knopps breathed deeply and surveyed the land, looking forward to the next seven days of adventuring.

After half an hour passed, Hagan still hadn't returned to shore on the skiff. Knopps began to fear that something had gone wrong. A full hour later, he was certain something had gone wrong. Through the scope of his rifle, he peered out to the sea and saw nothing but the larger boat bouncing in the waves of the harbor. Hagan and the skiff were nowhere to be found.

After still another hour had passed, Knopps feared the worst. Weeks later, his suspicion would be confirmed when Garret Hagan's body washed ashore miles down the coastline. The overloaded skiff had capsized in the frigid harbor waters and Hagan had drowned, just as Knopps suspected.

As if the death of his friend wasn't enough to process, Knopps realized he had other troubles to deal with. Without the skiff, and with half a mile of hypothermic saltwater between him and the main boat, he was stranded in some of the world's most remote wilderness. On top of that, the tide was rising quickly.

A deeply religious man, Knopps held a short impromptu memorial service for his friend and began moving inland to find protection from the rising tide. In less than an hour, the grassy plain between the icy river and the sheer rock cliff would soon be covered in frigid saltwater. He considered walking farther inland toward the treeline next to the rocky cliff. But as night fell, he knew those trees would be crawling with wolves and bears that were not at all afraid to prey on humans.

Fortunately he had another option. Knopps found refuge in the upturned roots of a large, dead tree that had fallen in the middle of the open plain. There would be no room to lay down, or even to sit down, but standing on these roots perched four or five feet off the ground, would at least allow him to stay dry.

That is, until it started raining.

The first drops began falling on Knopps in the early evening, and continued unabated all night and kept on throughout the following day. Clad in only a light windbreaker jacket with nothing but four granola bars to munch on, Knopps assessed his situation. He and Hagan had planned to be in the remote wilderness for a full week, so friends and family wouldn't even notice they were missing for seven more days. After that it would be at least another day or two before the Coast Guard would label the men officially "missing" and begin searching.

He reasoned that he could eat one of his four granola bars each day until Thursday, and then survive with no food for the remaining three or four days. It wouldn't be pleasant, but it would be survivable. He looked out again toward the harbor where the anchored fishing boat still danced softly in the waves. He breathed a small sigh of relief knowing that this boat would eventually give away his location to the rescue helicopters flying overhead when they came searching for him the following week.

After his first full day in the elements, Knopps watched in disbelief as the tide that evening rose more than a foot higher than it had the night before. At high tide the next day it rose another foot higher still. At first, Knopps thought his eyes had to be deceiving him—that's just not how tide systems work. But later that night, the clouds broke just long enough for him to catch a glimpse of the moon. Sure enough, it happened to be a full moon that week, which was pulling the tides abnormally high. By Wednesday night, the water was just inches below his foothold on the fallen tree.

And rain. Still more rain.

Mercilessly, the rain continued to fall, just as it had for the previous three days and nights.

On Thursday, Knopps nibbled away his last granola bar looking out at Hagan's fishing boat still bouncing in the harbor, as he tried not to think of his aching feet. Exhausted and uncertain whether he could remain standing through another night, he tied himself around the tree with his belt so that he wouldn't fall off the tree and into the water.

Just when Knopps began to think that things couldn't get worse, the clouds grew even darker and a wind gust came roaring in from the harbor, nearly blowing him off his perch. In an instant the persistent rain that had tortured him all week transformed into a howling thunderstorm. More powerful gusts followed, blasting him for five to 10 minutes at a time, every few minutes for the next 48 straight hours.

Finally, in the early morning hours of Sunday—a full week since he became stranded—the storm relented. The wind died down. The rain stopped. The clouds departed.

But Adrian Knopps' nightmare was not yet over.

When the sun came up later that morning, nature revealed its twisted sense of humor. Knopps looked out to the harbor in a mixture of disbelief and horror. The fishing boat that he and Hagan had arrived on seven days before—the aerial landmark that had been his best hope for salvation all week—was gone. The intense winds the night before had ripped the most visible marker of his location off its anchor, and set the boat adrift aimlessly out into the sea.

It was then that Adrian Knopps succumbed to the grief that he had so diligently kept at bay all week through a combination of prayer and perseverance. He climbed off the upturned tree roots and laid flat on the ground in a state of utter despair and incomprehensible exhaustion. As he closed his eyes, his hope faded with the light.

●

Most of us will never have to endure the kind of ordeal that Adrian Knopps did.

But on a different scale, changes of all varieties can sometimes make us feel like we're stranded—whether from the arrival of a sleepless baby at home, a new competitor in your market, a painful divorce, a devastating illness, the loss of a job, or yet another stifling government regulation levied on your department. Often it feels like all these things happen at once. You want to lash out at the universe and scream: "Really? Now you're just piling on!"

And just when we start lamenting our sense of isolation or helplessness, we feel that first raindrop land on our nose. Then another and another and another, until we find ourselves trapped in a driving rain with gale-force winds slapping our faces and stinging our eyes. In these moments, it becomes awfully tempting for even the most resilient people among us to wonder what we did to deserve all this.

In times like these, I find it's helpful to remember the Taoist story of the old farmer who had worked his crops for many years, and had only one horse left to call his own. One day, the farmer's only horse ran away.

His neighbors said, "I'm so sorry. This is such bad news. You must be so upset."

The stoic farmer just said, "We'll see."

A few days later, his horse came back with 20 wild horses following. The farmer and his son corraled all 21 horses.

His neighbors said, "Congratulations! This is such good news. You must be so happy!"

The farmer just said, "We'll see."

A short time later one of the wild horses kicked the man's only son, breaking both his legs.

His neighbors said, "I'm so sorry. This is such bad news. You must be so upset."

The farmer just said, "We'll see."

The country went to war, and every able-bodied young man was drafted to fight. The war was terrible and killed every young man, but the farmer's son was spared, since his broken legs prevented him from being drafted.

His neighbors said, "Congratulations! This is such good news. You must be so happy!"

The man just said, "We'll see."

And so it was with Adrian Knopps. Barely an hour after he laid down on the soggy grass, resigned to his fate, he awoke to a loud buzzing sound. When he opened his eyes, he could hardly believe what he saw.

A helicopter.

●

Against all odds, the Coast Guard had come looking for Adrian Knopps Sunday morning, even though it was still half a day before anyone expected Hagan and Knopps to return to civilization in the best of circumstances. The Coast Guard would have given them at least another 24 hours to come home before officially declaring them "missing." So what brought them there now?

It turns out that when the wind ripped Garett Hagan's enclosed fishing boat off its anchor the night before, it drifted down the coastline, where it was spotted by a pair of fishermen who were miles away from Knopps. The fishermen then reported the crewless boat to the Coast Guard around three a.m. The vicious wind that had attacked Adrian Knopps without mercy for three straight days was the exact same force that ultimately triggered his search-and-rescue effort three days ahead of time.

We'll see.

And what about the rain? That steady, unrelenting rain that started falling just hours after Knopps became stranded and continued tormenting him for the next seven days? In hindsight, it also turned out to be a blessing. Rainwater that pooled in the crevices of the tree turned out to be the only source of fresh water available to Knopps all week after the rising tide surrounded him in a sea of saltwater. As any survival expert will tell you, fresh water is infinitely more important than food for preserving life and health while stranded in the wild.

We'll see.

On the other hand, what about the fishing boat anchored in the harbor? Knopps viewed the stationary boat as the symbol of his salvation all week. As long as that boat stayed put, he reasoned, he stood a good chance of being rescued. He prayed that it would stay exactly where it was. In reality, the boat drifting away turned out to be the best thing that happened to him. It might have been the very thing that saved his life, as there were no guarantees he would have been able to hold on for another three days. Had his desperate prayer been answered, he might not have survived.

We'll see.

I wonder if there is a lesson here for the rest of us about more effectively leading change?

I wonder if, sometimes, the harsh winds and the constant rains are actually conspiring to *help* us instead of to harm us— even though we can't see exactly how in the moment? I wonder if some of the boats we cling to for salvation in the beginning might serve us better in the end if we let them get ripped free of their anchors?

We'll see.

The truth is that sometimes the winds of change *blow*—both literally and figuratively. Sometimes a series of unfortunate events put us in a place we'd really rather not be. Sometimes those changes put us in a position that, by all objective measures, simply sucks. But just as often the events we curse the most end up being the events that bless us most. Sometimes change blows, and it's a good thing.

A few weeks after he returned home to Michigan, Adrian Knopps granted an interview to a local radio station. At one point, the interviewer asked the even-keeled Knopps how he made sense of the strange series of events that ultimately led to his rescue. Knopps reflected quietly for a moment. "I guess you never know," he said. "You never know if your enemy is your friend."

Change is a lot like that.

NOTES: LIES, DAMNED LIES, AND CITATIONS

•

•

GENERAL NOTES

1. **Nick's imaginary friends.** All the stories about clients I've worked with, or research that we've conducted, are real. To protect the innocent people and sensitive information, I have gone to great lengths to disguise names, places, functions, job titles, industries, and any other details that might identify the real people on whom these stories are based. If you happen to recognize someone you know in here, it is completely by chance. To make it a more memorable and less snooze-inducing reading experience for you, I've chosen to use fictitious proper names of people and places rather than ambiguous pronouns. For example, instead of saying "the sales manager at that company," I've chosen to say "Glen Peterson at Davis Medical." But you can rest assured knowing that

the key details of each story—especially the instructive details—are derived from real people in real situations.

2. **Sins of omission.** You'll notice below that some chapters are missing from the notes. The reason is simple: Not all chapters required notes. So rest assured that when, for example, I skip from Chapter 3 to Chapter 6 to Chapter 8 in the notes below, it's not because your book is defective. It's because this book and my melon are the sources for Chapters 5 and 7. So no notes are necessary.

●

CHAPTER 1: SANDY'S RULE

1. **Communication isn't the problem.** Sandy's revelation that her repeated communications seem to have fallen on deaf ears is surprisingly common. In a study published in the March 2015 issue of the *Harvard Business Review*, researcher Donald Sull at the London School of Economics found that middle managers were four times more likely to cite a large number of corporate priorities as a barrier to executing change, rather than lack of clarity in communication. In other words, repetition and frequency of communication wasn't the problem for those lower in the organization. It was the fact that the leadership failed to make enough decisions about what is and what is not priority.

2. **Loss aversion.** The term loss aversion was first introduced in the 1970s by Amos Tversky and Daniel Kahneman in their 1979 article "Prospect Theory: An Analysis of Decision under Risk" in the journal *Econometrica*. I devote a few chapters to it in my first book *The Impulse Factor* (Fireside, 2008). The best and most accessible update comes from the 2011 book *Thinking, Fast and Slow* written by the man himself, Daniel Kahneman.

3. **Gorillas on film.** You'll probably be just as shocked as I was to learn that this study was not in fact inspired by Duran Duran's hit single *Girls on Film*. Fear not, however, there is still a reference to 1980s pop culture to be found here. The title of Daniel Simons and Christopher Chabris' 1999 article, in which they published their findings, is "Gorillas in Our Midst: Sustained Inattentional Blindness for Dynamic Events." I'd like to take this opportunity to

thank Sigourney Weaver for her immense contribution to behavioral science. If you want to know more about the gorilla study, be sure to check out Simons and Chabris' fascinating book *The Invisible Gorilla* (Crown, 2011).

●

CHAPTER 2: WHY THE PRINCIPAL KILLED THE FOOTBALL TEAM

1. **Premont High School.** Probably the only thing more remarkable than Premont's historic decision to nix football is how much press coverage the decision received. That this decision was newsworthy at all speaks volumes about the immense value (and some would argue overvalue) that American society places on high school athletics in comparison to high school academics. I first learned about it in Amanda Ripley's 2013 article "The Case Against High School Sports" published in *The Atlantic*. (Any guesses where Amanda Ripley falls on the academics vs. athletics debate?) Some of the quotes came from her article, while others came from a 2012 *Texas Observer* article "The Writing on the Wall" and a piece in the *Corpus Christi Caller Times* called "Friday with no football."

2. **Trick cards.** Bruner and Postman's study was reported in "On the Perception of Incongruity: A Paradigm" first published in 1949 in the *Journal of Personality*.

●

CHAPTER 3: DRIVERS AND PASSENGERS

1. **Are you a driver or a passenger?** These 12 questions make up the "Core Self-Evaluation Scale." This is a shortened version in comparison with the much longer original. This one has been reduced to include only the most statistically predictive questions. However, if you were to use this for screening people—either for selection or classification as many companies do—you should contact Tim Judge, now at Notre Dame's business school at tjudge@nd.edu or look him up at http://www.timothy-judge.com to get his guidance and to make sure you're using the right version for your specific need.

2. **Decisions create happy illusions here, and also happy outcomes there.** "Effects of Mindset on Positive Illusions" by Shelley Taylor and Peter Gollwitzer was published in 1995 in the *Journal of Personality and Social Psychology*. Whether George Washington created positive illusions for himself by micromanaging the renovations on Mount Vernon or by leaving that job to the copious amounts of tobacco he grew we'll never know.

●

CHAPTER 6: WHO'S THAT BEHIND YOU?

1. **Different people, different decisions.** If you really want to understand why people have different decision styles, my entire first book, *The Impulse Factor*, was devoted to explaining the research on that topic. It covers everything from genetics to environment to fleeting situational variables and how all those factors have come together to shape human civilization for roughly the past 40,000 years, from the first cave paintings all the way to the bursting of the housing bubble in 2008. It's pretty comprehensive and also pretty interesting . . . although I might be a tad biased.

2. **Estee Lauder.** The story of Freda Fabrizio's successful change effort at Estee Lauder comes from Shawn Tully's "An Outsider in the Family Castle" published in the October 13, 2013 issue of *Fortune*.

●

CHAPTER 8: SERIOUSLY, WHO KEEPS MOVING MY CHEESE?!?

1. **A cheesy mystery.** For the uninitiated, *Who Moved My Cheese?* (Putnam, 1998) was Spencer Johnson and Ken Blanchard's wildly successful parable on organizational change. That plus John Kotter's *Our Iceberg Is Melting* (St. Martin's Press, 2006) pretty much defined a decade of business in which the only thing bigger than organizational change was anthropomorphism.

●

CHAPTER 9: PIVOTS AND POWER STROKES

1. **The quick brown fox jumps over the lazy dog** is a phrase that uses every letter in the English alphabet. With a little Internet sleuthing I discovered that this phrase is called a "pangram." I thought I'd share that just in case you ever find yourself in a life-or-death match of *Trivial Pursuit: World's Least Useful Words Edition*.

●

CHAPTER 10: START WITH ~~WHY~~ 13½ PERCENT

1. **Playing with LEGOs.** The details of LEGO's turnaround come from Wharton professor David Robertson's fascinating account in *Brick by Brick: How LEGO Rewrote the Rules of Innovation and Conquered the Global Toy Industry*. It's a great analysis of the leading methods of innovation and why each one failed to produce results on its own, but also how a strategic combination of different methods finally saved the company. Even if you're not a business geek, if you are a LEGO geek you'll probably find the history of the company and its iconic products interesting enough to invest the time in reading it.

●

CHAPTER 12: THE REVOLUTION THAT WAS TELEVISED

1. **The Sopranos.** For the inside scoop on *The Sopranos* I relied mainly on Brett Martin's fascinating telling in *Difficult Men: Behind the Scenes of a Television Revolution*. If you find the entertainment industry or any of the new crop of television shows that seem to dominate the tube these days interesting, you'll love this book. Although I didn't touch much on this angle, Martin's book and the television revolution as a whole contain a number of great lessons about innovation. The 2014 bidding war for HBO and its astounding balance sheet come from the July 2014 *BusinessWeek* article "Buying Time Warner to Get HBO's Money-Making Machine."

●

CHAPTER 13: THE PULSE, THE ANTI-YOU, AND THE MINDSET

1. **Mickey Mouse + Barbie.** Mattel's decision to sponsor *The Mickey Mouse Club* comes from Ruth Handler's own telling in her autobiography *Dream Doll* as well as the June 6, 2005 issue of *Fortune*.

●

CHAPTER 15: TO LEAD IS TO DECIDE

1. The story of Rich Lloyd's decision on the morning of the Oklahoma City bombing comes from the book *Built from Scratch: How a Couple of Regular Guys Grew The Home Depot from Nothing to $30 Billion,* written by The Home Depot's co-founders Bernie Marcus and Arthur Blank.

●

CHAPTER 16: ROSA PARKS AND THE SCIENCE OF REVOLUTION

1. **Claudette Colvin's courageous ride** and her subsequent relegation to the backseat of the Civil Rights movement come primarily from Phillip Hoose's book *Claudette Colvin: Twice Toward Justice* and Fred Gray's autobiography *Bus Ride to Justice: Changing the System by the System, the Life and Works of Fred Gray* (revised edition).

2. **Mobile middle, edgy elites, rebel yell.** I pulled from a number scholarly works to arrive at the fundamental elements that make or break revolutions, including Crane Brinton's *The Anatomy of Revolution*, James DeFronzo's *Revolutions and Revolutionary Movements*, John Foran's *Taking Power: On the Origins of Third World Revolutions*, and Erica Chenoweth and Maria Stephan's *Why Civil Resistance Works: The Strategic Logic of Nonviolent Conflict*. As a history buff and a social science geek, this was probably my favorite chapter to research and write. In fact, when I originally set out to write *Domino*, the entire book was going to be about the science of revolution and how it pertains to changes in

organizations, individuals, and society as a whole. Timing wasn't right for that book right now, but perhaps some time in the near future? Stay tuned. . . .

●

CHAPTER 18: MOBILIZE THE MIDDLE

1. **The myth of the 21-day habit.** In 2012, psychologists at the Health Center of University College London attempted to set the record straight by aggregating research from their lab and others. They tracked down the book by Dr. Maxwell Maltz, who is believed to be patient zero for the habit myth, and then traced its path to modern research on the topic. You can find the resulting explanation of their search online at https://blogs.ucl.ac.uk/hbrc/2012/06/29/busting-the-21-days-habit-formation-myth/. The scholarly article on the topic was published in the *European Journal of Social Psychology* in 2010 under the title "How Are Habits Formed: Modelling Habit Formation in the Real World."

2. **The working memory limitations debate.** Princeton psychologist George Miller's classic 1956 study, "The Magical Number Seven, Plus or Minus Two" in *Psychological Review*, was the original work on the limited capacity of working memory. It was a pretty big discovery at the time, and it was a very valid conclusion based on the evidence Miller had to work with. For an update on the subject, the best place to go is probably University of Missouri psychologist Nelson Cowan's 2005 book *Working Memory Capacity*. The study of working memory capacity is an inexact science because of all the confounding variables and difficulties in experimentally distinguishing between working memory and long-term memory (e.g., memorizing someone's phone number is actually more about long-term memory than short-term memory), and whether memorizing letters is the same as memorizing words, which may or may not be the same as memorizing numbers or faces, and so on. All of that notwithstanding, it's universally agreed that the true capacity of the average person's working memory is probably three, four, or five items at a time.

●

CHAPTER 20: THE HARDEST PERMISSION TO GIVE

1. **The endowment effect** was a term coined by University of Chicago behavioral economist Richard Thaler in his 1980 paper "Toward a Positive Theory of Consumer Choice" in the *Journal of Economic Behavior and Organization*. I devoted a whole chapter to it in *The Impulse Factor*. Much of Thaler's work and its practical implications are summed up in the fantastic book he wrote with his colleague Cass Sunstein, called *Nudge: Improving Decisions About Health, Wealth, and Happiness*.

●

CHAPTER 21: PRIORI-TIME: THE ANTIDOTE TO URGENCY

1. **How and why priori-time works.** In a series of experiments in 2013, published under the title "Neural Reactivation Links Unconscious Thought to Decision-Making Performance" in *Social Cognitive and Affective Neuroscience*, psychologist David Cresswell of Carnegie Mellon showed that when we start thinking about a problem or a decision, and then are forced to turn our attention to another task for a while, our brain keeps evaluating the relevant information behind the scenes. To be sure, the impact of unconscious thought is still a murky and hotly contested field among researchers right now. For our purposes, though, it doesn't matter much whether the processing is truly unconscious, partly conscious, or completely conscious. The point is simply that *it works*. The periods of distraction can help us make better decisions about the high-priority items as long as we prime ourselves to think about that prioritized topic.

●

CHAPTER 23: SCIENTIFIC MANAGEMENT 2.0: FROM TAYLORISM TO TASLERISM

1. My favorite manifestation of this new mode of management is *The Lean Startup* by Eric Ries. Don't be misled by the title—this isn't about cost-cutting methodology, and it is every bit as useful

for *Fortune* 100 companies as it is for startups. If you've recently heard the terms "minimum viable product (MVP)" or "build—measure—learn" or "vanity metrics" or "a pivot" and wondered where it came from, wonder no more. Eric Ries is your guy. And Eric Ries's guy is Steve Blanck who is basically the intellectual forefather to this new movement. His book is titled *The Startup Owner's Manual*.

INDEX

•